BETTER POLICE ETHIC

Dedication

To the memory of Andrew Nicholas Graeme Somervell, killed on military service in Northern Ireland in 1973: a staunch comrade and a good friend.

BETTER POLICE ETHICS:
A PRACTICAL GUIDE

Peter Villiers

KOGAN
PAGE

The masculine pronoun has been used throughout this book. This stems from a desire to avoid ugly and cumbersome language, and no discrimination, prejudice or bias is intended.

YOURS TO HAVE AND TO HOLD
BUT NOT TO COPY

First published in 1997

Kogan Page Limited
120 Pentonville Road
London N1 9JN

© Peter Villiers, 1997

British Library Cataloguing in Publication Data

A CIP record for this book is available from the British Library.

ISBN 0 7494 2164 9

Typeset by BookEns Ltd, Royston, Herts.
Printed in England by Clays Ltd, St Ives plc.

CONTENTS

PREFACE

Better Police Ethics is for the working police officer who confronts ethical dilemmas every day. He or she is an intelligent, busy, practical person, not necessarily versed in moral philosophy, who wants something to act as guide, philosopher and friend. Parliament has codified police behaviour in investigating crime under PACE, the Police and Criminal Evidence Act of 1984, but it cannot codify ethical behaviour. Ethics is about choice. However, it should be informed and thoughtful choice.

Better Police Ethics is written to be logical, comprehensive, helpful and stimulating. The text should be easy to read, and I have tried to make it friendly without being patronizing. I have imagined myself as sitting down (or up) with a colleague, discussing these problems, and then writing up (or down) my conclusions.

This book is written to be read from start to finish, and each chapter builds upon its predecessor. If you wish to read it in another order, for example by starting with the chapter on case studies, then please do so. You may miss something, but the book will still make sense in whichever order it is read. There are some recommendations for further reading at the end.

The text is interspersed with activities: dilemmas, problems and things to think about. The moral dilemmas which appear in the text have been written as both realistic and generally applicable – the sort of problems, in other words, that you might come across, but which you do not normally have much time to reflect upon. How should you answer them? With your shoes off, and without anyone peering over your shoulder – unless you want them to. There are no right answers to these dilemmas, in the sense that there is a right answer to a mathematical or logical puzzle. There are, however, degrees of adequacy in the ways that they can be answered, and the commentaries bring out underlying issues.

Anyone who writes a book about ethics has to ponder his own moral position, and to reflect upon his motives for committing his views to paper. If I have any understanding of the subject, it is from a lifetime of trial and error: with the emphasis upon error. Why, then, am I writing about it? When I was taught mathematics at school, the master was young, gifted, and impatient. Clearly adept at every form of calculation himself, he could not understand how anyone else could fail to grasp what he understood so easily. Consequently, he was a poor teacher; and I later learned my arithmetic from a less brilliant scholar who was able to understand my difficulties. Is this, then, a book in remedial ethics? Certainly not: but it is clearly applied rather than pure.

I was brought up in the Church of England, and in a lifetime of both active and passive resistance I have been unable to shrug off that pack. Indeed, as I have grown older I have returned to the teachings I once rejected. If I were a character in *Pilgrim's Progress*, I should be called Mister Has-To-Work-It-Out-For-Himself. In this book I make a connection between religion and ethics which you may not accept. No matter: if we can agree or disagree on a constructive basis, then I shall have achieved my objective.

ACKNOWLEDGEMENTS

To the friends and colleagues from my life – personal, military, police and academic – who have influenced my moral development for better or worse, and of whom this list is an inadequate survey:

Robert Adlam, Jeannine Alton, Jonathan Bailey, Michael Barclay, Pamela Bourgein, Andrew Coid, Alasdair Dennis, Ronald Flanagan, Roger Gaspar, John Grieve, Peter Heier, Tania Jarosowa, John Kleinig, Roger Lindsay, James McKinney, Thomas Maguire, Walter Merricks, Francis Murray, Robert Nairac, Jonathan Pattenden, Steven Peover, Charles Radford, Neil Richards, Alan Ryan, John Slater, Andrew Swarbrick, Raymond White, John Wilson and Robert Woodward

To the library staff, who have been unfailingly friendly, helpful, and professionally incurious. And finally, to the many police officers who furthered my education at Bramshill Police Staff College when I was supposed to be teaching them, and whose patience and good humour has helped us through many a long hour.

ABOUT THE AUTHOR

Peter Villiers lectures at the national Police Staff College in Hampshire where he has worked since 1986. He has trained a large number of senior police officers both from the United Kingdom and elsewhere, and is responsible for ethics training amongst other subjects. From this unique perspective, he has benefited greatly in his understanding of police decision-making.

Peter Villiers studied government at Essex University and organizational psychology at Lancaster, and has carried out post-graduate research into occupational stress. During an extended short service commission in the army he served in Hong Kong, Northern Ireland and Cyprus, where he worked as a liaison officer for the British contingent of the United Nations Force during the Turkish invasion of 1974.

Peter Villiers has had considerable experience of working alongside and with police officers and is keenly aware of the nature of the moral dilemmas they face. Indeed, such is his interest in the subject that during the mid-1970s he was working as a liaison officer to the RUC in Northern Ireland and at the same time attending evening classes in moral philosophy at the University of Belfast. Perhaps unethically, he did not share his real identity with his tutor.

He is also the author of two other books, writes frequently for police and other magazines and undertakes consultancy assignments.

1
THE PRESSURES OF POLICE WORK

PRESSURE

On 15 July 1992 a young mother was savagely attacked and murdered on Wimbledon Common in London, in the presence of her not quite 3-year-old son. The murderer got away unseen. The case generated enormous interest and concern, but the police had no very clear leads. From a description of a man seen near the scene of the crime, they produced a photofit which bore some resemblance to a 29-year-old single man living on the Alton estate, just off the Common. His name was Colin Stagg, and he was interviewed by the police as a possible suspect. Nothing emerged. Stagg remained on file, and the police continued their enquiries.

Mr Paul Britton, a psychologist who had helped the police on various occasions and was known to be able to create an 'offender profile', was asked to assist the inquiry and did so. The profile he created – in other words, the picture of the sort of man who might have carried out this crime – had some points in common with Colin Stagg. The police, said Mr Britton, should be looking for a lonely, inadequate, and sexually inexperienced person, capable of carrying out his sadistic sexual fantasies, which were of a particular type. The total number of such men in the population would be small.

To create an offender profile is one thing: to obtain a conviction, another. Was Stagg the man? How could the police find out? In the absence of forensic evidence, they needed a confession. Stagg was known to have struck up a correspondence with a woman through a lonely hearts club, until she broke off the relationship because she was disgusted by what he wrote. A detective came up with the idea of enticing Stagg to reveal his fantasies through a manufactured contact.

. . . .

If Stagg could be persuaded into correspondence with a suitable person, then he might be encouraged to reveal his inner self, which could give evidence linking him to the Wimbledon murder, or clear him of it.

The detectives carefully considered the proposed ruse. If they were able to obtain evidence by means of its use, would a judge accept it? After all, they were setting out to deceive Stagg. The plan might be considered to be a form of entrapment, and any evidence gained by its use inadmissible in court. What were they to do?

. . . .

ACTIVITY

You will probably have read about this case, or remember something about it. Suppose you knew only what you have read so far, and were in charge of the investigation.

1. Would you authorize an operation in which a police officer were to become Stagg's correspondent, build up a friendship with him by letter, and attempt to gain evidence which would implicate him in the Wimbledon Murder, or clear him?
2. On what basis would you make your decision?
3. If you approved the operation, how far would you allow the correspondent to go? Would you allow her to write what she liked, or would you impose limits?
4. What difficulties might arise in running the operation?

Comment

1. Authorization

For the operation
You might decide that this sort of operation sounds acceptable enough. After all, if Stagg is innocent he has nothing to fear. No one can force him to write what he doesn't want to. You may not like the idea of hoodwinking someone, playing with his fantasies, and generally leading him up the garden path, but these things are occasionally necessary. After all, we are investigating a murder, aren't we? And this will be a

very carefully controlled operation. We shall be committing the small evil of invading a man's privacy and deceiving him, for the much greater good of solving a crime, and possibly preventing its repetition. In other words, the end justifies the means.

Against it

On the other hand, you might decide that the operation is unjustified and the tactics it will involve are bound to lead to trouble. In exploring someone's sexual fantasies you would be wading in some very murky water, and the exercise might strike you as not only distasteful but extremely difficult to manage. In the torrid emotional climate that you would be setting out to create, how would you be able to distinguish between fact and fantasy? What judge or jury would accept anything that came from it?

2. The basis for the decision

It can be extremely difficult to say when, how and why a particular course of action is decided upon. The normal framework for decisions includes the following.

Precedent

If a method has been used before, its further use may be less controversial. Although the details of this case may be unique, the ploy is not original.

Risk: worst case scenario

It is sensible to estimate the risk of any proposed course of action before taking it. Here, it would be wise to consider what would be the worst way in which the operation could go wrong, and whether or not the police could cope with that situation, or less extreme variations of it.

Cost-benefit analysis

This is a variation on the above, wherein you consider what you hope to gain, estimate what you will have to lay out to achieve your aim, and decide whether or not it is wise to proceed. Costs should not be considered purely in financial terms.

Moral reasoning

Explicit moral reasoning may be rare, but any important decision will usually attract moral statements, although they may not be classed as such. An example would be a remark such as: 'How would you like it to happen to you?'

Authority

Although it cannot be a substitute for clear thinking, it is both sensible and comforting to appeal to a recognized or higher authority to endorse a decision already made, or guide the group towards consensus if no conclusion has been reached.

3. Limits

Clearly, this operation would need to be carefully controlled. What might appear a reasonable risk at the outset could easily develop into something very different.

4. Difficulties

A very large number of difficulties could emerge. For example:

- ☐ *Control.* Risks could arise that had not been anticipated or considered, to do with the dynamic relationship of the two parties.
- ☐ *Cost.* Deception plans are expensive.
- ☐ *Inconclusiveness.* Suppose Stagg started to reveal things which might be significant, but were still ambiguously phrased. Would you carry on, or stop at a given point? What given point?
- ☐ *Discovery.* As well as sometimes proving expensive, lengthy and inconclusive, deception plans tend to be discovered.

The police took advice from the Crown Prosecution Service, who indicated no objection to the proposed method of gathering evidence. They then went ahead and set up an elaborate and in the end very expensive operation whereby a carefully chosen policewoman wrote a series of letters to Stagg, advised in their creation by the helpful Mr Britton. The operation succeeded in the sense that Stagg was convinced that he was genuinely in correspondence with someone who shared his sexual fantasies, but it failed in that over a lengthy period of time he did not reveal anything which tied him to the murder of Rachel Nickell. During this time Stagg met his correspondent four times, and received a tape-recording as well as letters.

Stagg was charged with murder on the basis that he matched the offender profile and that the fantasies he revealed in correspondence with policewoman x made the possibility that he was not the murderer 'vanishingly small'. The words were those of Mr Britton, in support of the prosecution's submission that there was a case to bring before a high court jury.

No case went to jury. Mr Justice Ognall reviewed the evidence and threw it out, on two grounds. First, it was entrapment. Secondly, it failed to produce the goods. The tactics used, said the judge, amounted to:

> A blatant attempt to incriminate a suspect by positive and deceptive conduct of the grossest kind. A careful appraisal of the material demonstrates a skilful and sustained enterprise to manipulate the accused.... Designed...to manoeuvre and seduce him to reveal fantasies of an incriminating character and to, wholly unsuccessfully, admit the offence.

Altogether, he condemned the operation as thoroughly reprehensible. No charges were pressed against Colin Stagg. He was declared clear, and at the last report was considering suing the Metropolitan Police for false arrest.

Review: the pressures of police work

We have explored the Stagg case in some detail, not simply because it went wrong or (arguably) demonstrated unethical behaviour, but because it illustrates a number of points about the reality of police work and the pressures it creates.

First, the police have an extremely important job to do. This was an horrific murder, and needed to be solved – not least because the murderer might well strike again.

Secondly, police work of this kind brings immense pressures, both from outside the organization and within it. The public expects the police to solve serious crimes, and the media attention is enormous. The senior police officers who manage police resources want results. Large sums of money are invested, which could have been spent elsewhere. Professional reputations are at stake.

Thirdly, it is difficult for the police to sustain their official role as the cool, scientific and detached investigative branch of the criminal justice system, testing a series of hypotheses as if they were attempting to isolate a killer germ. Police work is not scientific in that sense, and never will be. We expect detectives to be good at their jobs, and that means becoming involved in what they are doing. It means having a feel for who might be guilty, and getting inside their minds. It means, on occasion, thinking like a criminal. Small wonder that in this case it was the police, and not the psychologist, who came up with the lonely hearts ploy. It is the police who are closest to the victim of a crime, or his or her surviving relatives. Be it robbery, arson or rape, it is the police, rather than journalists, lawyers or probation officers, who see the suffering caused.

Fourthly, it is an accepted procedure for the police to test the system. Lord Justice Ognall rejected the evidence presented to him as inadmissible; but he might not have done. After all, the CPS considered the method legitimate. The stipendiary magistrate considered that there was a case to answer. Another judge, it could be argued, might have accepted the evidence; and who knows what a jury would have made of it? It is not for the police to judge people, but to put the evidence before the system, which is precisely what they did.

Fifthly, police work builds up a momentum, which becomes difficult to stop. Once Colin Stagg had come into the murder enquiry, he had to be convicted or eliminated.

Finally, it has so far proved very difficult for the police to create a body of knowledge based upon the systematic analysis of a series of case studies, by means of which to improve their professional skills. Police work in general, and especially the investigation of crime, is traditionally regarded as a craft; and craftsmen do not share their skills except to their chosen apprentices. Every case is described as unique, and few attempts have been made to synthesize what has been learned and to present it as a body of knowledge or set of doctrines which can be taught to all initiates. What we are touching on here is the underlying reality of police work and the pressures it creates; and that deserves a separate section.

THE NATURE OF POLICE WORK

Ordinary and extraordinary

The bobby on the beat is, or should be, the cornerstone of British policing. Much of what patrolling police constables do is distinctly ordinary. The presence of the police officer is both a deterrent to crime and a visible reassurance to law-abiding citizens. The officer, in many cases, does not necessarily have to do anything. He just has to be there. On the street corner, where the youths would otherwise congregate. In the town centre, where people have frequently complained that they never see a police officer. In the market where stolen goods are sometimes sold, pockets picked, and regulations evaded; and some traders have been known to comment that they have seen rather too many police officers. On the face of it these duties do not sound very onerous, and to an office or factory worker who may be doing something repetitive and tedious, they may sound very attractive.

> What? Do you mean to say, that you're paid to walk up and down and **talk** to people? And if they offer you a cup of tea, you can have one? I wouldn't mind your job, mate!

Suppose that a child has gone missing. The anxious parents cannot find her, and they appeal to the police for help. A search needs to be organized and carried out. Organizing such a search is largely a matter of common sense, for it involves doing on a larger scale what we should all be capable of doing in miniature. Sensible questions have to be asked, and plans made. For example:

- Is the child really missing, or is she hiding under the bed?
- When was she last seen, and by whom?
- In terms of her normal habits, where might she be?
- Who are her friends, and what do they know?
- What does she look like? What was she last seen wearing?
- How many people are available for the search, and for how long?
- Where will you base the centre of your search?
- How will you divide up the ground?
- How will you communicate with the searchers?

Clearly, there are better and worse ways of addressing all these subsidiary tasks, and an experienced police officer should be able to make a better job of organizing the search than a novice. If specialist equipment or training is required to search particular areas, such as rivers, mines or factories, then the police officer will need to be able to organize and coordinate this. Nevertheless, in terms of the professional skills required, this is an ordinary task; and a police officer is a citizen in uniform who does by virtue of his calling what any citizen might be minded to do as a matter of conscience or social responsibility.

Why, then, do I start with the fundamental premise that police work is extraordinary? Partly because police work deals with moral issues, and involves the constant, instinctive evaluation of peoples' motives and character. Take the missing child. Why did she go missing? How long did the parents take to report it? Is there an issue of child abuse here? Probably not. Over-suspiciousness is a fault in itself, and not to be encouraged. Children do go missing, and many cases are speedily and happily resolved; but the good police officer is both active in his ostensible professional duties – ie organizing the search – and at the same time professionally curious as to what he may uncover. When confronted with an absorbing task, many people would forget themselves in it, if only for a time: but the police officer must always keep part of himself back.

An inner voice is always whispering in his ear:

There may be more to this than meets the eye ...
This doesn't smell right ...
This person may be lying ...

A police officer, whatever his rank, has to rely upon his own judgement and his own instinct for what is right, and he can only develop that instinct and judgement over time. At the same time, he needs to develop (for none of us is born with it) the professional double identity which enables him to be both active participant and cool, detached observer. Until he has mastered this, or if at any period of his working life the two halves of his personality, as it were, are not synchronized, then he will not be able to be both ordinary and extraordinary.

Police officers as ordinary citizens with extraordinary powers

Police officers are neither supermen nor wonderwomen. They are not the product of a Platonic scheme to produce a class of guardians, bred and trained over generations to be dispassionately wise and just in all that they do, and to act only in the interests of society as a whole (as articulated by Plato). We may select, train and supervise our constables and senior officers as much as we like, but we are still working with fallible beings. Indeed, we claim the ordinariness of British police officers as one of the great strengths of our system of policing. British police officers represent the society which they police. They are not the product of a traditional elite, such as the public schools or the older universities. Formal educational requirements are very low. Training is comparatively short and mainly practical: police officers are not being prepared for membership of a learned profession, but to make swift, practical, robust decisions on the streets. The work requires physical strength and endurance, patience, determination and resilience; and these are the characteristics that will be looked for, more than intellectual skills.

Power and its misuse

The police are in a position of both authority and power. Whom do we set out to flatter, influence or corrupt? People who hold power. With power, hopefully, comes responsibility. With power, certainly, comes the possibility of its abuse. Power corrupts, said Lord Acton; and the officer of the law may be corrupted into not using his powers, as well as using them wrongfully. The police are the executive arm of the criminal justice system. Their action or inaction may dictate someone's future, for good or evil. It would be extremely surprising if they were *not* subjected to unethical pressures. These may range from a request to ignore a parking offence, to a plea not to be prosecuted for something much more embarrassing: and the person asking for a favour or exemption may be able to exert great pressure. This can lead to unethical behaviour – after all, it is easier to concede than to resist – and it can also lead to a sort of generalized cynicism about human nature which may have unethical consequences.

Knowledge is power (and power corrupts)

The police officer sees people operate under pressure, and is able to see the weakness in a public figure whom others can only observe (and probably admire) from afar. He has seen that person on the spot, and knows something of the reality lying behind the image. The professional police officer looks for the weaknesses in people, whether or not he has any immediate need of that knowledge. The fundamental problem for the police officer is whom to control, and whom to support; and a knowledge of any deficiency will enable him to pursue either policy more effectively.

The world's a stage ...

If social life can be compared to a drama, then the police officer is what is called in the trade a 'character actor'. He plays a supporting (or destructive) role in regard to other actors, who may be more prominent, but whose impact depends upon his support. He is either on stage or backstage; he is no longer, once he has taken his oath, a member of that frivolous, enjoyment-seeking, innocent group of people to be found in the auditorium.

Backstage, the police officer is like the dresser, who sees the great actor with his guard down, and may be required or at least expected to take part in unethical activities in order to disguise the greater immorality of his master. For example, consider the active social life of various American Presidents, whose womanizing has been hidden, assisted or protected by their bodyguards. I do not, of course, wish to address my remarks more particularly than that!

Police officers' ambivalence about their work

Philip Bonifacio (1991) writes from a psychodynamic perspective and confines his observations to male North American police officers. His work is based upon the insights of Sigmund Freud, rather than the measuring tools of social science, and its validity is open to question. Before we question it, however, let us see if his thoughts are of sufficient insight to merit questioning. Bonifacio's argument is that police work creates great pressures upon its practitioners, because of the sort of people they are. As a good Freudian, he is sure that those pressures are the more pernicious for being unappreciated or denied at a conscious level.

Why is police work so pressurizing, in his view? Because it creates, or rests upon, a fundamental ambivalence. To be ambivalent about something is to love and hate it at the same time. Many of us are ambivalent about our work, but police officers are particularly so. Bonifacio suggests that this is because police work is inevitably disillusioning. Police officers, he suggests, go to the police academy because they wish to do something to help people. They are highly trained for a concentrated period, and then graduate from the academy and become patrol officers. Almost immediately, as they realize the chaos and decay that is life on the streets, disillusionment sets in. Police officers realize that they cannot reform society, and that the opportunities which they have to do real, practical good are extremely limited. This causes ambivalence, all the more dangerous if it is unacknowledged or suppressed.

Bonifacio further suggests that police officers do not only feel ambivalent about their work, but much else besides. They feel a mixture of love and hate for the police organization, their colleagues, their families, and themselves. Much of this conflict, or ambivalence, is either repressed or denied, at the conscious level. However, the pressure is there, and it leads to inappropriate and dysfunctional behaviour. For example, a traffic policeman who tends to display a hostile and aggressive attitude to drivers whom he stops, makes his task of enforcing the law and improving driver behaviour more difficult. As in other situations, we are likely to see a self-fulfilling prophecy here. The disillusioned and ambivalent police officer assumes that the driver to whom he is about to speak will be rude and uncooperative, and frames his behaviour accordingly. The result? The behaviour he had anticipated in the first place! If a police officer is ambivalent about his work, then he may be more susceptible to pressure to behave unethically.

Analysis

Bonifacio's thesis is cogently written and intuitively plausible. As a Freudian explanation it is largely unfalsifiable, since it posits that unconscious forces may control behaviour. If a police officer says that his experience has *not* made him ambivalent, then the Freudian psychoanalyst may simply say that the officer has repressed his ambivalence to a sub-conscious level. Unfalsifiable explanations, according to Popper (Magee, 1968) are unscientific, and have no validity; if they are true, it is by coincidence. The well-known British psychologist H J Eysenck has taken this much further, and in his book *The Decline and Fall of the Freudian Empire* (1986) suggests that Freudian theories of personality are unhelpful from start to finish. I think that this goes too far, and that Freudian explanations of behaviour are worth considering within a context of healthy scepticism. In this case, it is possible to test the ambivalence theory, since it may be the case that some police officers will not have suppressed their ambivalence, but will admit to feeling disillusioned about their work and alienated both from it and society.

Many surveys have shown that police officers do feel cynical and disillusioned about their work, to a greater extent than other people in the public service. We have still not proved, however, that cynicism or alienation necessarily leads to unethical behaviour. It is plausible to speculate that it might: but plausibility is not proof.

....

— If he's getting away with it, why shouldn't I?
— Everyone's corrupt, really. The thing is not to get caught.
— We never finish the job, do we? Every time we arrest this kid, the magistrate slaps his wrist and says he's been a naughty boy. Come to think of it, she doesn't even say that, now. Then the social worker wants to know if he could discover himself on adventure training in the Bahamas. Well, let's try some adventure training here, shall we? Let's see if he can dodge this brick.
— I don't know why I bother. I work bloody hard in this job, and then I go home and get slammed by the kids. Am I responsible for the behaviour of every policeman and woman in this country?

A model of police behaviour

The model of police behaviour being put forward here is that the new police officer passes through various stages, which can be labelled as follows:

- ☐ Initial enthusiasm.
- ☐ Contact with reality.
- ☐ Disillusionment.
- ☐ Cynicism and alienation.
- ☐ Unethical behaviour.

We now have a choice:

Either
- ☐ further contact with reality which reinforces cynicism
- ☐ downward spiral of unethical behaviour and influence
or
- ☐ renewed but more realistic enthusiasm
- ☐ modulated contact with reality
- ☐ good behaviour.

Supposing that there is some validity in this model, the problem for the police organization is to ensure that the virtuous cycle is pursued and not the vicious one. How is this to be achieved? It is at this point in the discussion that someone will usually bleat out the word 'training', as if that were the panacea for any problem. I should prefer to start earlier.

FACTORS FOR AND AGAINST ETHICAL BEHAVIOUR

So far in this book we have been considering the pressures on police officers which the work imposes, the effects it has upon the personality, and the unethical behaviour which may result: as if the process were inevitable.

'Join the police', we seem to be saying, 'and you'll find it all too much for you. And then look what will happen! Don't say we didn't warn you.'

In reality, just as there are pressures upon police officers to behave badly, so there are pressures upon them to behave well.

Background factors and active measures

British policing is a system which has evolved over nearly two centuries, and the measures which we identify as acting as barriers to ineptitude, misbehaviour and corruption may not have been consciously designed in that way. Some have simply evolved. Policing is an organic process, not a mechanical one.

Tradition

The modern tradition of British policing is a fine one, and something to look up to, rather than a thing of which to be ashamed. (In passing, we must comment that a proud policing inheritance is far from true of many other countries, and is a considerable advantage to Great Britain.) The creation of the New Police by Sir Robert Peel in 1829 was a remarkable attempt to create a civil, civilized and civilizing force in the face of widespread disbelief and hostility, not just from the criminal classes, but from the British public as a whole. Britons associated policing with the heavily authoritarian practices then prevalent in countries such as France, and wanted none of it. Create a police force, they said, and you will create a police state. They were proved wrong. The British bobby was able to build a positive relationship with the British public and to lay the foundations for policing by consent. Like Roman legionaries, British police officers have a history, tradition and standard to follow.

While policing must evolve over time, changes need to be considered very carefully, and rejected if they are not conducive to the good. The traditional image of the British bobby is of a kindly, avuncular figure (masculine, it goes without saying) whose uniform bulges at the seams as he bends over to admonish some youthful tearaway. Both know the rules of the game, and there is no hostility in the picture. The bobby's protection, a helmet, is as much symbolic as practical; and his only weapon is a wooden truncheon, apologetically concealed. Sentimental as such an image is, it once had some basis in reality. Does it still? The avuncular village bobby is becoming a thing of the past – apart from anything else, he would probably fail the fitness standards that are now being enforced upon regular officers – but some of the values and traditions in which he believed are with us still. The uniform, equipment, gender and ethnic background of the police officer may change, but the public service ethos to which he or she subscribes, must remain.

Ethos

Ethos is hard to define. I see it as a collective ethic, a sort of highest common factor of what everyone believes. The ethos of the British police service is to be fair, compassionate and honourable. Not every police officer will reach those standards, and some will fail spectacularly, but the ethos is there.

Selection

In theory, if only you could select the right officers for your police service, then you need take no further action. Ideal police officers would be infinitely fair, compassionate and honourable, and policing could be safely left in their hands. Indeed, if we pursue the fantasy to its logical conclusion, we need not even worry overmuch about the recruiting process. Ideal police officers would have a vocation for policing, and would join the force whatever the obstacles placed in their way. Recruiting officers would simply have to announce vacancies, provide information, and check for the occasional case of a mistaken calling.

This ideal need not detain us overnight. First, no human being is perfect. Secondly, the police service does not have a total command of whom it may recruit. People who might have made excellent officers may be recruited by other organizations with which the police cannot compete. Should the ideal police officer have a vocation? Maybe: but there will be many good police officers who did not. The police service needs to recruit the right people, and the more successfully it can do this, the fewer the ethical problems it will face. Selection will never be perfect, but that is not a reason to abandon a policy of continuous improvement.

Selection in action

The United Kingdom has a large number of separate police forces. Despite various coordinating mechanisms such as national police training, there are significant variations in recruiting policy. It is not my purpose in writing a book on police ethics to lay out an ideal recruiting policy, but to make some comments as to where ethical considerations and recruiting criteria meet.

The tradition of police recruiting is a fairly rough and ready one. Many of the original recruits to the New Police in 1829 were sacked within a year, often because of drunkenness on duty. Gradually a system evolved which, although far from scientific, met the requirements of the service. Police recruiting has generally emphasized disqualification rather than qualification. If a police service had vacancies, you could join provided that you met the minimum standards. A police officer had to be of a certain size, weight and strength, and in good health. Although there were no formal educational requirements such as O or A levels, he had to demonstrate basic literacy and numeracy. But what about his aptitude for the work itself, and his moral and spiritual capacity to cope with the pressures it might impose? Any criminal record was a disqualification; and the criminal record of his family would also be considered, not on a presumption of genetic criminality but because of the pressures which criminal relatives might exert. (In the British police service, unlike in many others, a potential police officer will not necessarily be excluded because he has close relatives in jail.)

Beyond that, moral qualities were assessed informally. The recruiting officer would make enquiries at the candidate's home and school and anywhere he had worked, and form an estimate of his character. Some things would count for a person, and some against; and no doubt a good recruiting officer could do a reasonable job on the basis of personal experience and judgement. He might even exert a more active role, and try to persuade some people to join the police whom he saw as having excellent potential, but who had not considered it. Essentially, police recruiting, like most aspects of police work, was practised as a craft, and if you saw a good piece of wood, you kept your eye on it. Not every promising sapling grew into a straight tree.

Aspects of the old system still survive, and police recruiting remains a local business with national guidelines. Preconceptions as to who could make a good police officer have been reviewed. Police forces have been making very serious attempts to increase the number of (suitable) women and members of ethnic minorities in the police service. Women have had a very insecure history in police recruiting, and blacks and Asians have hardly been recruited at all until very recently. Although obstacles remain, that situation is now changing. The logic of setting out to recruit more women and members of ethnic minorities to the police force is severalfold:

☐ First, it goes against prejudice, and since prejudice is by definition irrational, that must be a good thing.

☐ Second, it allows the police to represent the society they police, and that should, other things being equal, make policing easier. Clearly it supports the philosophy of policing by consent.

☐ Third, it allows the police to recruit from a wider pool. This means that selection can be more selective, and that people who would not traditionally have taken to police work, but who have excellent moral standards, may join and apply them. Am I being optimistic? Yes, certainly. And why not?

As always, change presents new problems, and the pressures of success may equal or succeed the pressures that arise from failure. Changes in recruitment have given rise to moral and practical issues which need to be addressed rather than ignored, and some examples follow in the case studies which are explored in depth later in this book, particularly to do with the recruitment of ethnic minorities and women.

A LAW-ABIDING AND PEACEABLE SOCIETY

A police service represents the society it polices and from which it is recruited, and the quality of British society will influence the quality of the police service it fosters. How can we evaluate so broad a topic as the quality of society, or compare one society with another? What evidence could be quoted in support of the hypothesis that our society is, in either absolute or comparative terms, law-abiding and peaceable: and what evidence could be offered to go against or disprove it? In case you were still wondering, these are rhetorical questions. Not only do I not know the answers to them: I am not sure where to look. The official ethos of the British, in so far as we have one, is that Great Britain is a liberal democracy which enshrines and practises the values of tolerance, fair play and self-restraint; and our national symbol is cricket. 'Move along, sir', says the bobby, and the by-stander moves along. George Orwell wrote of the gentleness of the English and of the English way of life; and comparisons are often made between, for example, the safeness of life in Great Britain and the violence of the United States, the tendency of the French to become over-excited, or the strange inability of the Germans to form an orderly queue.

We could easily drive a coach and horses through any of these generalizations. You do not have to be a paid-up member of the Militant Tendency (should they accept anything so capitalist as money) to recognize that Great Britain is often a violent, exploitative and dangerous society; and any historian will be happy to demonstrate that we have an extremely riotous past. Our behaviour overseas is telling. After the Indian Mutiny broke out in 1857 we dealt with the ring-leaders by lashing them to cannons and blowing them asunder. (James Morris, one of the coolest of writers on our imperial past, refers to this in terms of the blood-lust of the race.) In 1919, when he considered that there might be a second mutiny, Brigadier General Dyer shot dead about 380 unarmed Indians in Amritsar in ten minutes. (With true military passion for detail, we know that, although certain other facts are unclear, 1650 bullets were fired. See Townshend, 1986, p. 137.) Dyer regretted that he was unable to use his armoured cars, since the entrance to the killing ground was too narrow for them to pass.

These are extravagant examples which occurred in an imperial setting. As far as events at home are concerned (and in this context I must refer to Great Britain and not the United Kingdom, which includes Northern Ireland), most social historians would seem to agree that for the past 50 years Great Britain has been a comparatively peaceful society. Most of our police officers still work unarmed. Riots are infrequent, and the exception rather than the rule. The proportion of police to the population as a whole, at about one to 500, is comparatively low. While various pundits have opined that respect for authority is breaking down, any historical analysis will reveal that this is what pundits have always said, and that there has always been a Golden Age, some 30 or 40 years ago, which we can never quite recapture.

In the end, there is no alternative but simply to assert that we *are* a comparatively calm and peaceable society; that it is to the advantage of our police service that we remain so; and that at least the more astute police officers are aware of the value of this tradition and the contribution it makes to better policing.

CONCLUSION

In this chapter we have reviewed the pressures upon police officers to behave unethically, and contrasted them with some background factors which help the police to maintain a certain level of good behaviour – but do not guarantee it. Can one be an ethical person in an unethical society? That is a question for you to keep in mind throughout your reading of this book. In the meantime, it is time to explore the fundamentals of ethics.

2

THE FUNDAMENTALS OF ETHICS

. . . .

ACTIVITY: OPERATION TORCH

Instructions

Please read the following story carefully, noting your reactions as you read it. It is about a police use of firearms which goes wrong. You are asked to keep the following in mind:

1. *Procedures*. This is a fictitious scenario, and although events like the one described have occurred within the United Kingdom – particularly where, as in Northern Ireland, the police routinely carry and use firearms – you might wish to claim that it could never happen in your force. That, with respect, is not the point. Please accept this story as something which *could* happen, and analyse it accordingly.
2. *Legal and moral responsibility*. In the questions that follow you are asked to evaluate responsibility. Please take this in the moral rather than the legal or constitutional sense.
3. *Questions*. Bearing the above in mind:

   ☐ Who is most to blame for what happens to Constable Abel?
   ☐ Who should be held responsible for the event?
   ☐ What does this story tell you about ethics and values?

Scenario

When Sergeant Doolittle arrived for work that morning he was not in a good mood. His inspector was away on a course, his wife was sick, and he had discovered something in his son's bedroom that looked suspiciously like pot. It was with a feeling of something like relief that he entered the battered nineteenth century monstrosity that constituted Police Headquarters in the decaying urban sprawl of Waterside (population 1.2 million, 40 per cent of adult males unemployed).

His pleasure at being at work was soon obliterated when he received a telephone call from an old source. Barry MacMenamin, known on his file as 'Jehovah', wanted to see him urgently. Doolittle sighed. Barry always wanted to see him urgently. The information he offered, convincing enough at the time, had somehow never proved usable when the time for action came. Detective Sergeant Doolittle wondered for a moment if he should have laid such store by this source. Barry had never actually been proved wrong in anything he said, and his reason for attempting to betray his colleagues in the criminal fraternity to the police was invariably the entirely understandable urge to increase his short-term income, but this did not prove the truth of his information. On this occasion, Sergeant Doolittle decided to go along with his source. He had very few informants, and even a spurious credibility was better than none. He had no urge to return to uniformed duties. Sergeant Doolittle put his doubts away and went to meet his source.

That afternoon he sought an urgent interview with his Chief Inspector, and subsequently a short meeting with the Assistant Chief Constable, whose permission was needed for the operation they had in mind. Permission was easily obtained. The ACC, Mr Stanley Goodchild, was a youngish man in a hurry, both in his career and on that particular afternoon. He had been promoted to his present rank in Waterside two weeks before, having previously attended a number of courses at the Police Staff College at Bramshill, and had no knowledge of Waterside, its criminals or its police force. He saw no reason to doubt what Sergeant Doolittle – in the presence of his Chief Inspector Saul – had to tell him, and in fact his questions were framed in such a way as to build on Sergeant Doolittle's information, rather than expose it to objective analysis.

At 6 o'clock that evening the firearms team was briefed. The briefing lasted seven minutes, and no one asked any questions. Present were Chief Inspector Saul, Sergeant Doolittle, the Firearms Team Commander and four constables. The team should have consisted of the Firearms Commander and six men, but two men were off sick; the unit had been understaffed for some time, and had no reserve.

Chief Inspector Saul set the scene. Information had been received that armed criminals would be in a house at Leese Avenue, Waterside, that night. There would be two men, armed with shotguns and pistols. They would not be expecting trouble, and would not resist arrest if taken by surprise.

Chief Inspector Saul ceased speaking (Sergeant Doolittle had said nothing at all) and the Firearms Team Commander, Inspector Abraham, set up his plan. Two men, Cain and Rossellini, would approach the house from the front, and the other two men, Abel and Tasman, from the rear. All four were to be armed with Heckler and Koch sub-machine guns surmounted by night vision devices of the latest type, supplied by the Army. The 'A' team of Cain and Rossellini were to enter the house and engage in a room-by-room search, preserving surprise until the last possible moment. The 'B' team were to take up position by the back door and remain there, acting only to arrest the two criminals should they flee. All movements would be silent. Trainers would be worn. Radio silence was to be preserved. Were there any questions?

Constable Tasman would have liked to ask not one, but many questions about this plan. Although new to the Waterside Police he had previously served for three years as Inspector in the RHKP and had taken part in a number of armed raids of the sort they were about to undertake. He did not like the plan at all, for he felt it offered far too many opportunities for error. However, he had only just joined the Waterside Police, and had already been reprimanded for questioning orders too often. Inspector Abraham was popular with his men, because he was always prepared to share whatever hardships were on offer, but he had never been noted for his capacity to gather their opinion on any plan he articulated before it went into action. In fact, his preferred management style was wholly autocratic, and Tasman held his tongue.

Constable Abel kept his peace for another reason. He was wondering if he would have a marriage to go back to, after the operation was over. His wife had been threatening to leave him for some time, and a succession of all-night operations with the FT Unit was proving the last straw. One more night away would probably mean a note on the table, an empty house and an even more irritating smile on the face of Constable Rossellini. Constable Abel was so preoccupied by his own thoughts that most of the briefing passed him by.

Constable Cain understood the plan very well, and was excited. They were to raid a house in Leese Avenue, and he was to lead the assault. He gripped his notepad more tightly and felt a constriction in his chest where he had forgotten to breathe. He had no questions.

The team were kept at HQ that evening, for security reasons. At midnight they bundled into a transit van, and by 1.00 am the two teams were in position. The house was silent as a wreck on the bottom of the sea. Inspector Abraham wanted to check it out with a night vision scope, but unfortunately none of the four scopes was working. They had been faulty ever since delivery, and although he had complained strongly about it nothing had been done. Had his unit been at full strength, then he could have detailed a man to look after equipment, but that had been impossible. As it so happened, he had asked another inspector to pursue the matter, and had written him several notes about it: but although Inspector Dark acknowledged his notes punctiliously, nothing had actually happened. Inspector Abraham looked through the device and realized it was useless. He told the four men not to use them, and set back the beginning of the operation by five minutes to allow the team's eyes to become accustomed to the darkness.

At 1.15 am precisely Constable Cain effected a silent entry to the house and began to check the first bedroom. All was quiet, and there was no sign that anyone had been there. He and his partner checked the two front bedrooms with extreme caution, then relaxed slightly. It was unlikely that anyone was at the house: and fat old Sergeant Doolittle had been proved wrong once again. Constable Cain moved into the hall and towards the kitchen. He came to an unexpected obstruction, and stopped to discover precisely what it was.

At the rear of the house, Constable Abel felt cold, tired, bored, hungry and miserable. He had had nothing to eat or drink at the station, for to do so would have meant going to the canteen, where someone would have been bound to ask him about his wife. He had no real interest in their operation: six minutes had gone by and it was obvious that the house was clear. He wished he were anywhere but there. Then he heard a sudden noise from the house, and forgetting his orders stepped forward to investigate. The rear door was unlocked and, brushing off Constable Tasman's restraining hand, he stepped into the house.

Constable Cain saw his armed silhouette in the faint light of the open doorway and immediately opened fire.

Commentary

If we look at this story from the legal point of view, Constable Abel should not have disobeyed his orders and entered the house. By doing so, he contributed to his own fate: and he must share some of the blame, and responsibility, for what occurred. Again, from the legal point of view, Constable Cain must be held to account, since he pulled what was presumably the fatal trigger. (Of course, his shots may have missed: but let us assume maximum drama.) Morally speaking, we can cast the net far wider. Rather like the characters of an Agatha Christie novel before Hercule Poirot sorts them out, everyone has some reason to be considered guilty. Let us deal with each of them.

Sergeant Doolittle

Sergeant Doolittle has something to answer for, and has more than lived up to his name. His motives for running his source have more to do with his own interests than the needs of the organization, and he is not an exemplary sergeant. On the other hand, he is not responsible for the command of the operation which was based upon his information.

Chief Inspector Saul

He is a far from impressive middle manager, who interprets his duties extremely narrowly.

Assistant Chief Constable Stanley Goodchild

ACC Goodchild has neglected his responsibilities shamefully, and could have been much more vigorous in his inquiries as to what was really going on. He was content to act as a sort of human rubber stamp, rather than to justify his position, status and salary by adding value to the chain of command. If you believe that the most senior person has the greatest responsibility for what occurs, then Goodchild is the worst offender.

....

Inspector Abraham

Inspector Abraham could be a better team leader in many ways.

Constable Tasman

Constable Tasman shows a lack of moral courage in failing to challenge the obvious demerits of the plan for the operation. He knows that any objection he raises is unlikely to be listened to, and may well have a career-damaging effect, at least in the short term. Either through prudence or fatalism, he does nothing; neither is a sufficient reason for inaction.

Constable Rossellini

Constable Rossellini's behaviour is open to interpretation! From an absolute moral standpoint, the story appears to suggest that he is an immoral person, and his immorality may have contributed to what happened.

Constable Abel

Already discussed.

Barry McMenamin

Should we exempt a source from moral criticism? Why?

Others

Other people could share the blame, to some extent: for example Inspector Dark, who appears in neglect of his duty to check and rectify equipment. His behaviour, too, contributed to the final result. We have neglected to mention Mrs Abel, who may have been indulging in an adulterous affair with the egregious Constable Rossellini. Are we going to exempt her from moral examination?

General remarks

Sergeant Doolittle's dilemma introduces the subject of ethical analysis by means of an operational example. It may cause us to reflect that:

☐ Considering a question of moral responsibility is a way into considering our general moral code.

. . . .

☐ Legal and moral responsibilities are related, but are not the same.
☐ What constitutes moral responsibility is a very deep issue, on which our views may well differ.
☐ The most interesting question is, perhaps, what is to be done?

. . . .

WHAT IS ETHICS?

It is time to lay out some maxims. Please note that in this book I shall continue to use the words 'ethics' and 'morals' and their derivatives as synonymous.

Ethics is about right and wrong

Is it wrong to steal?

This is clearly recognizable as an ethical question. It is phrased in grand terms, with the implication being that stealing under any circumstances must be either right or wrong.

Is it wrong to steal bananas?

This is clearly a lower-order question. If it is wrong to steal, then it is also wrong to steal bananas. This raises the issue that there may be degrees of wrongness. Stealing bananas from a supermarket may be thought less wrong than stealing a senior citizen's only source of vitamins. Stealing bananas from anyone may be thought less wrong than stealing their iron lung machine.

Is it wrong to eat bananas?

This does not, at first sight, look like an ethical question, nor even a sensible one. What could be wrong with eating bananas? But this question is also phrased in terms of right and wrong, and is therefore set in the ethical arena. Some people think it is wrong to eat meat; and no doubt someone, somewhere, is starting a banana liberation front. Something is an ethical question if it is declared to be so. How important it may be is another matter.

Ethics is about making defendable choices

Should you eat bananas from Dogmatica?

If by eating (or, more importantly, buying) its produce you help to
support the economy of a corrupt despotism, then you may consider
that you should not do so.

In a liberal democracy we would normally assume that moral choice
is an individual and indeed often a private affair. Unless the
government chooses to ban imported goods or produce from a
particular source – in which case the choice has been made for us –
then it is up to us as individuals to decide what to do. We may take a
firm moral stance, and refrain from buying a certain item – as, for
example, many people abstained from buying South African fruit during
the era of apartheid.

On the other hand, we may persuade ourselves that our action is
unlikely to have any real affect, since it is a drop in an ocean; or that we
shall be harming the Dogmatican fruit-growers if we boycott their
produce, and not the corrupt politicians who have already salted away
their profits in Genevan banks or the Austrian post office system; or
that there are other and more effective ways of protesting Dogmatican
behaviour than by boycotting their fruit.

We might even argue that we support Dogmatica and wish to buy
their fruit in preference to fruit from elsewhere. However, unless we
wish to be perverse we are unlikely to claim we wish to support a
despotic and corrupt regime. We are more likely to suggest that the
Dogmatican government has been misunderstood; or that the
chattering classes do not give it credit for its firm stand against
communism; or some other argument which indicates that our
position, too, is based upon principle. As we warm to our case, we
may assert that our principle is one which we have thought about more
carefully than the anti-Dogmatica brigade, with their thirst for
confrontation and simplistic, sloganized approach to complex issues.
But here we are straying from ethics into rhetoric – a distinction to
which I shall return. Essentially, ethics is about making defendable
choices of behaviour.

Ethics is about courage

– You can't really believe that ....

— I should never have thought it of you ....
— Now I know who my real friends are ....
— Are you in this team, or aren't you?
— This is how we do things here.
— This is not a moral issue. It's a practical one.
— That might be the sort of thing they talk about in training ....
— We don't have time to debate it. Are you in or out?
— You do realize the consequences, don't you?

Ethical dilemmas are not trivial. They arouse controversy. People may argue passionately for one solution or another: look at the debate about abortion in the United States. Adopting and sticking to a position may make you unpopular, ostracized, unemployed, imprisoned, tortured or dead. It may also make you admired or loved.

Courage, heroism and leadership

In many cases, courage, heroism and leadership are linked, so that we would be hard put to separate them. John Keegan (*The Face of Battle*, Penguin, London 1978) refers to Captain Sparks of the London Scots and his conduct in the battle of the Somme. I quote:

> *The burden of managing the fighting now fell wholly upon (the last surviving company commander) Captain Sparks. 'The better to direct the fighting, he was often seen standing and moving on the unbroken ground between the trenches' – conduct which would have attracted admiration at Waterloo, and when displayed on a First World War battlefield, beggars powers of eulogy. By 4 pm Captain Sparks recognized that his tiny force, now under attack by thirteen different German infantry companies from three different regiments, was about to go under. He sent the following message back across no-man's-land:*
>
> 'I am faced with this position. I have collected all bombs and cartridges from casualties. Every one has been used. I am faced with three alternatives:
> (a) to stay here with such of my men as are alive and be killed.
> (b) to surrender to the enemy.
> (c) to withdraw such of my men as I can.
> Either of the first two alternatives is distasteful to me.
> I propose to adopt the latter.'
>
> *Using discarded German rifles and ammunition, he and four N.C.O.s made a final stand in the German front trench while the other survivors escaped into no-man's-land. There most of them, including Sparks, hid until darkness fell and allowed them to regain the British lines. During the*

day the London Scottish, which had numbered 856 at dawn, had been reduced by death or wounds to 266.'

By contrast, Leon Villiers (*The War on the Workers*) refers to a solitary act of certain self-sacrifice. He tells the story of a steam engine-driver whose train crashes and who releases the steam from the boiler lest it explode and kill everyone. The only way in which Driver Goodchild can render the boiler safe is to release the steam over himself, and his death will be both agonizing and inevitable. No one is there to witness his act of self-sacrifice, and no one would blame him if he held back. Nevertheless, he does it.

Physical courage is what people show in the face of physical danger, whereas moral courage is required when one faces the more insidious enemy of isolation. In the case of the Driver Goodchild, the two overlap. Both require belief in oneself. Physical courage can be akin to recklessness, although pure recklessness, as Aristotle pointed out, is not a virtue: if you are not afraid of something then you do not have to conquer yourself to face it. Captain Sparks was not reckless. What he did was necessary for a leader in battle, and his letter is a remarkable example of coolness under fire. The person who faces physical danger may have had time to prepare himself to face it, in which case his body will have produced adrenalin to raise his energy and confidence in the expectation of violent effort; but adrenalin is neither necessary nor sufficient for the manufacture of courage. The truly courageous person is he or she who can calmly and level-headedly face up to danger, having considered the possibilities, and being prepared to risk or sacrifice himself either to save others, or simply to carry out his duty.

An heroic police service?

In the police context there are many opportunities for the exercise of discreet and unlauded heroism. The service requires its officers to display quiet, steadfast resolution in the face of danger every day: but it is not usually the sort of display which leads to citations and medals. It is interesting to note that while London bristles with statues to heroic soldiers, sailors and airmen, no heroic police officers are immortalised in bronze; and although there is a statue to Lord Trenchard, he is remembered as Marshal of the Royal Air Force and not as a vigorous and reform-minded Commissioner of the Metropolitan Police. When police constable Yvonne Fletcher was shot dead outside the Libyan Embassy in London in 1984 and the film director Michael Winner suggested that her death, and others, should be commemorated, there was no overwhelming enthusiasm for the idea – although it has now been done.

In the same context, it is interesting to compare the atmosphere of the army's staff college at Camberley with those of the police staff college at Bramshill. Camberley commemorates our military past, and its paintings, silver and other memorabilia celebrate the virtues of courage, duty and sacrifice as shown by the officers, non-commissioned officers and men of the British army. Many of the portraits are of famous generals or other soldiers, and the underlying message is very clear: the British army is proud of its past, present and future, and in no doubt as to what it represents.

The police college, on the other hand, makes much less of the past, and has no heroic portraits of police officers doing their duty – although compassion is portrayed. One of the more interesting artefacts is a totem-pole-sized statue of a police constable who is not actually doing anything at all: he is just *there*, policing the foyer of the gymnasium. Any officer visiting Bramshill will see group photographs, plaques and gifts from foreign police forces galore: but he will see little evidence of what the police service believes in and stands for, to compare with Camberley.

Some, no doubt, would see this as a good thing. Armies and police forces are not the same, and a self-consciously heroic police service would have little contact with ordinary peoples' hopes, aspirations and fears. But the gap is there. What do the police believe in? What are their cardinal virtues? Is courage acknowledged? The answer is yes, but in a very British way: one we might call unheroic heroism.

When interviewed, police officers are often very off-hand about any dangers they may have faced, and will make remarks such as:

– It's all part of the job.
– I was only doing my duty.
– Anyone else would have done it.
– Would you excuse me, please? I have to get back to work.

If possible, they will inject humour into the situation, which helps to imply that they are just ordinary people who happen to be in the right place at the right time. If one reads accounts of police actions, this is obviously untrue. The following extract, written in decidedly unheroic language, illustrates my point.

Even though he is a modest, friendly and unassuming man, Inspector Gary Boughen seems to be a magnet for assorted cranks who want to throw punches at him. The first time it happened, he nearly died.

On 24 April 1994 while making an arrest outside a fish-and-chip shop in Edlington, a district of Doncaster, the then Sergeant Boughen suffered a beating with kicks and punches that broke his nose, fractured two cheek bones, closed both his eyes, smashed the infra-orbital bones around his eyes, caused his face to swell massively and left many bodily bruises where the boot had gone in.

That brutal and unprovoked attack earned Inspector Boughen a nomination for the Brave Officer of the Year Award sponsored by the Police Federation and *The Sun*.

(Police Magazine, July 1996, p. 34)

The article goes on to say that this officer suffered some permanent injuries from his attack, but is still on police duty and is still facing the same sort of confrontations in a run-down inner-city area.

Inspector Boughen's devotion to duty, I would suggest, is not untypical; nor is his modesty. The police service would prefer recognition for its general achievements than star status for individual officers. The service was originally modelled on the army, and still has aspects of the military culture. Trainee police officers are expected to drill, salute, polish their shoes, and wear their uniforms smartly. As I write, they still have passing-out parades. If they carry out their duties conspicuously well as serving police officers, they will be commended for it by a judge or chief constable, or simply by a letter of thanks from the public. Some police officers are recognized in the national honours system; and anyone who can last 22 years receives a long service and good conduct medal – which comes up with the rations. But while exceptional deeds are recognized, it is durability that really counts. It is the police officer who goes out to do his duty again and again, despite discomfort, fear, pain, ostracism, and on occasion despair, who is the real hero.

The account in *Police* implies that Sergeant Boughen was acting alone. Had there been colleagues within reach, they would have had a duty to support him. They would not have known why he was being attacked, nor why he had been making an arrest in the first place. In the heat of the moment such considerations are irrelevant. They are issues which can, if necessary, be looked into later. What counts is action.

Because of the risks and dangers of active policing, police officers must support their colleagues to know that they will be supported in their turn. As in the armed services, comradeship is highly desirable and loyalty prized. Loyalty, however, should not be an absolute virtue. We all admire the person who goes to the aid of another at risk to himself. But if a police officer is doing something wrong, and expects another officer to support him, or at least not to denounce him, in the name of loyalty, then that is a perversion of an ideal; and the truly courageous officer will not support his colleague in wrong-doing.

To go against what a colleague is asking for, expecting or demanding – or, if a senior officer, ordering – requires moral courage of the first order. In the police service, which is effectively more a way of life than an occupation, and in which group norms are of extraordinary strength, it is an immense challenge. A police officer of any rank has a responsibility to uphold the law, directly to the Crown. In that sense, every police officer is a leader.

Ethics is about fundamental beliefs and values

Since not all ethical questions are phrased in terms of right and wrong, it may be necessary to bring out the ethical dimension underlying what appears at first sight a practical issue. The underlying dimension may be brought out by asking questions until no further explanation is available.

'Don't kill your neighbour.'
– 'Why not?'
'Because it's wrong to kill.'
– 'Why is it wrong to kill?'
'Because it would be a very bad state of affairs if we all went round killing each other. You wouldn't like it to happen to you.'
– 'I don't intend to go round killing a large number of people. I only want to kill Harry Smith. I shall do it very discreetly. That won't lead to an outbreak of copycat killings. Besides, no one's going to kill me. I know how to defend myself.'
'Well then ... You shouldn't kill your neighbour, because human life is sacred.'
– 'Why is human life sacred?'
'Because it is.'

That is an irreducible ethic. You cannot go beyond it. You may agree with it, or disagree. You may see it as a basis for civilized existence, or an outmoded shibboleth. What is clear is that it is an ethical statement.

. . . .

The religious connection

Christian teaching tells us that Man is made in the image of God, that we all have an immortal soul, and that we are all of equal value in God's eyes. That is a religious justification for the fundamental ethic that killing is wrong; and killing is explicitly forbidden in the Bible. We may, if it applies, take our fundamental beliefs to the religious level, and say that they rest upon the teachings of Christianity or another religion. However, to quote a religious justification for something is not to explain it further to others, unless they share our faith or we are attempting to convert them to it. We have simply rephrased our fundamental belief in religious language.

Human life is sacred because our religion says so

Some would argue that ethics and religion are indisseverable. It is more accurate to say that they are historically connected. Ethics need not be based on a religion, not even the substitute creed of humanism. It is possible to be an ethical atheist, and although the atheist's ethics may have originated in the teachings of a religious prophet, he is entitled to claim that he does not adhere to them for that reason, nor in hope of heavenly reward. The majority of people might find an ethical code too cold and abstract to accept, unless they could relate it to the more familiar teachings of a religion, and which give meaning to their life, suffering and death; but that does not mean that we cannot have ethics without religion. To believe that is to do justice to neither concept. Their inter-relationship is explored further in Chapter 9.

Ethics is about consistency

Ethical debate can only take place between people who accept the rules of debate. One of those rules is consistency. We expect people to be rational and consistent over time. If someone believes in the ordination of women on Tuesday, we shall expect him to hold the same conviction on Thursday, or to be able to explain why he has changed his mind. We do not expect people to be arbitrary in their opinions and attitudes.

Consistency is not enough – someone may be consistently wrong, as was Pol Pot in his attitude towards people who wore glasses – but it does offer predictability and allow for organized social life.

Ethics is about reciprocity

The Christian Golden Rule states that I should not treat others as I would not like to be treated myself. In positive terms, this is usually called: Do as you would be done by. This must be an incomplete basis for moral choice – after all, there must be occasions when I cannot know how I should like to be treated, or my choice might be arbitrary, odd, or frankly masochistic – but it is an important principle.

Ethics is about universality

– It might work. . . .
– Why don't you just try it? What have you got to lose?
– People probably won't find that out. . . .
– It's a tough old world. . . . That's what people do in business.
– You couldn't be expected to consider everything. . . .
– It was the best you could do under the circumstances. . . .

It is of the essence of a balanced and defendable judgement or choice, that we should be able to offer it as a solution on a wider scale than simply as the solution to problem x at time y. The philosopher Immanuel Kant described this principle in various ways. One version is as follows: 'I am never to act otherwise than so that I could also will that my maxim should become a moral law.'

Ethics is neither relative nor absolute

Ethics means making value judgements and living by them. It does not imply moral relativism. That is the credo that we have the right to make choices for ourselves, but not to criticize the choices of others, nor to attempt to influence their behaviour. By implication, ethical choice is a matter of taste. Some people like strawberries and others don't. Once we have found out whether or not another person's preferences coincide with ours, that is as a far as we can go. One choice is as good as another.

In regard to behaviour which obviously and directly affects other people, moral relativism is absurd. If I believe that murder is wrong, then how can I assert that this proposition does not apply to someone else? If murder is wrong, it is wrong for everyone. If I should not murder people, then nor should anyone else. What if someone else espouses a different set of values to mine, and believes that murder is right? Can we reconcile two such opposite views? Clearly not. It may be possible to acknowledge that in other countries, people do things differently; but that is to side-step disagreement, rather than to abolish it.

Suppose another country had a tradition in which murder were approved under certain circumstances. It would be no defence under English law, or generally accepted morality, to say that you had killed another man because you had been brought up under the Sicilian code of the vendetta, and that you had an obligation to kill in order to safeguard or restore the honour of your family. Nor would it be a defence to say that you had killed an alleged religious blasphemist such as Salman Rushdie in order to fulfil a *fatwa* – although that challenge has yet to come to court.

In a community which accepts the rule of law, some activities will be proscribed, whatever your religious, cultural or racial background; and they will not be confined to unlawful killing. Does this mean that ethical judgements are absolute? Not entirely. The notion of what is acceptable may change over time, especially in a world in which medico-technical advance poses new conundrums.

The role of the police officer in a multi-cultural context

What is the role of the police officer where cultures clash, and moral relativism beckons? It may be tempting for the police officer who is attempting to strike a balance in a multi-racial and multi-cultural society, to offer a position of apparent moral relativism on some issues. Up to a point, such behaviour is sensible. The police officer is not required to issue gratuitous condemnations of what he might have been brought up to see as immoral behaviour. He will wish to keep as much of the public on his side as he can, and one way to do that is to demonstrate that he is aware of differing beliefs, customs and values. Tolerance is a virtue, as far as it can be applied: but there are limits, to which we shall return.

Summary

Our maxims about ethics may be summarized as follows.

Ethical choices are important, and reflect our fundamental beliefs about right and wrong, which we can articulate and defend. Our behaviour should be consistent and when necessary, courageous. We ought to stand up for what we believe in, and we should not expect from other people what we do not offer them. Ethical standards are neither relative nor absolute. Ethics, religion and law are not coterminous – as we shall explore in examining how our maxims may be applied by police officers.

POLICE, LAW AND MORALITY

What are the police for? To enforce the law? To uphold morality? To keep the peace, which may mean condoning both illegality and immorality? Or are they simply an arm of the state, and the whole ethos of liberal democracy and its separation of powers an elaborate sham?

Policing takes place within a particular view of the world, whose assumptions may be so unquestioned as to be almost invisible. Great Britain proclaims itself to be a liberal democracy which accepts the rule of law. Writers such as Joycelyn Pollock (1994, p. 72) would suggest that the values of a liberal democracy are not superordinate, but may be seen as fitting within a consensus paradigm, as opposed to its opposite, Marxian, notion that society is based upon a conflict of class interests in which the economically powerful dictate what is legally and morally right.

Pollock illustrates her point as follows:

> (Consider the) difference between ... a mining accident and a multiple murder. Despite the same end result (dead victims) the mining company would probably go unprosecuted or receive very minor punishments for its role in the death of the miners. For the conflict theorist this would be an example of how law has been written differerentially to serve the interests of the power holders. The definition of what is criminal often excludes corporate behaviour, such as price fixing, toxic waste dumping, or monopolistic trade practices, because these behaviours, although just as harmful to the public good as street crime, are engaged in by those who have the power to define criminality.... Some would even go so far as to parallel corporate crimes and organized crime.
>
> (Pollock, 1994, p. 73)

In my experience police officers are very well aware of the comparative moral iniquity of various crimes. Their conduct is not guided by the unseen forces so dear to Marxist sociologists, but by the clearly rational motive of making inquiries which will lead to a result. The police officer's three guiding questions are:

1. Has a crime occurred?
2. Can we identify the perpetrator?
3. Can we place him at the scene of the crime?

These can be applied to any incident, but if we consider some so-called white collar crimes such as fraud, it is clear that the police have extreme difficulties in mounting quick, cheap and effective investigations, and can get results more easily elsewhere. The failures of the Serious Fraud Office illustrate my case. It is not necessarily unethical that the police should concentrate their efforts where they have a reasonable chance of a success: and if some types of crime are as a result comparatively neglected, then this is more because of inherent difficulties of investigation than through the active interference of the rich and powerful.

One of the consequences of policing by consent is that the police must follow rather than lead public opinion, in terms of what is acceptable. We might wish that more attention were paid to crimes that affect us all, rather than individual victims; but to encourage the police to decide their own priorities would open the door to zealots and zealotry. Having said that, the police could do more to review their policies, priorities and progress in the light of shifting public opinion in an age of single-issue causes and lobbyists. Police forces are essentially conservative, and the British have yet to follow the example of the Dutch or the Danes and invest significant thought and resources into the investigation of environmental crime. It is time they did so.

The good police officer

Should we have a notion of what makes for a good police officer? Is he simply someone who does his duty? If so, what is his duty, and who decides it? There is a strong potential for circularity about much of this, and some preliminary under-labouring is needed.

Imagine that you hear someone saying: 'She's a good police officer.' What does the phrase conjure up? I would suggest that your thoughts will probably have something to do with effectiveness. A good police officer is good at her job, however success in that job may be judged. She makes arrests when that is necessary. She investigates crimes successfully. She supports her colleagues. She does not shy away from the difficulties which go with police work, be they associated with boredom, fear or stress. There is a systematic ambiguity about the word 'good'. It could mean that someone is either good at something, or morally admirable, or both. In the case of the police officer, her worth is defined both by her actions and by what she stands for.

Good police work

To know what good police work should be like, we need to decide the product. What should the police produce? We can begin to explore this by considering arguments from authority as to why the police exist, what they are supposed to produce, and how their product or service is to be measured or evaluated.

The Royal Commission of 1962 described police duties in England and Wales as:

1. To maintain law and order and protect persons and property.
2. To prevent crime.
3. To detect criminals. In the course of interrogating suspected persons, the police have a part to play in the early stages of the judicial process.
4. To control road traffic and advise local authorities on traffic questions.
5. To carry out certain duties for government departments.
6. The police have by long tradition a duty to befriend anyone who needs their help, and they may at any time be called upon to cope with major or minor emergencies.

Since no Royal Commission has been held on the police since 1962, this is the last official definition of police duties.

The Government's White Paper of 1993, *Police Reform: a Police Service For the Twenty-First Century*, although lacking the status of a Royal Commission, expresses the government's views very clearly. It states that the main aims of the police service should be:

- ☐ to fight and prevent crime;
- ☐ to uphold the law;
- ☐ to bring to justice those who break the law;
- ☐ to protect, help and reassure the community;
- ☐ in meeting those aims, to provide good value for money.

In fulfilling those aims the police must maintain their traditional role of policing by consent. The exercise of police powers will continue to be separate from the exercise of police authority.

I cannot see that in essence this is so very different from what was said in 1962, with a shift of emphasis and an attempt at measurability. The military analogy that the role of the police is to *fight* crime is wrongly construed. The police are not simply there to fight crime; and even if they were the verb is misleading. Armies do not set out to fight, but to conquer. There is no merit in a long campaign, and a military operation should be a concentrated exercise in the shortest effective use of overwhelming force. That is *not* the basis for successful police work, which requires patience, humour and steadfastness.

Conviction or due process?

If we believe that the police service exists, at least partly, to assist the process of criminal justice, then we still have to decide how it is to fulfil that role. If it is the proper role of the police service to bring people whom it believes to be persistent or outrageous criminals to court, and to gather and present its evidence in such a way that there is a very strong likelihood that they will be convicted, then that demands a certain sort of behaviour and recognizes a certain set of values. Successful police officers in that context will be energetic, hard-headed, unsqueamish, flexible about rules and task-driven.

If, on the other hand, we believe that the proper role of the police service is to make even-handed inquiries into the background and circumstances of a crime, so that a proper conviction may be achieved if the evidence, fairly gathered, is sufficient – then that requires a different approach and a different set of values. The police officer becomes more like a scientist whose job is to examine the evidence and see in which direction it leads him, rather than to rely upon his intuition in reaching conclusions.

Traditionally, the British police service has inclined more towards conviction than due process. Is the service ready to embrace the other role? Does it believe in it? Is it right? The first two questions are empirical, and can only be answered by research. The third question is philosophical, and the consensus of opinion is that the role of the police should be to carry out their investigations in a professional manner, not only by observing the rules, but according to the spirit of what is intended under our judicial process. It is not the role of the police officer to break, ignore or twist the rules so that suspects become convicts. It is his task to research both crime and possible criminals as carefully as possible, and present his findings to the court.

Is it natural that a police officer should feel sympathy for the victims of crime, and hatred for those who prey upon the weak, the elderly and the otherwise vulnerable? I would say that both sympathy and hatred are perfectly natural. It is what is done with those emotions that counts. It is to the greater good of society that we have a police service that obeys the rules, rather than one which manipulates the system at the expense of its own ethos and credibility. The police must take the long-term view. That is the true meaning of professionalism.

Preserving the peace

Clearly, the police have a major role to play in preserving the peace. This can require frenetic efforts by specially trained squads but, to use a military analogy, once you put deterrence into action, you are acknowledging that it has failed. It is the existence of a stolid and stalwart constabulary which provides an atmosphere of security, rather than what it actually does. However much he might complain about them, it is the knowledge that the police exist which gives the citizen of middle England the sense of well-being in which he feels safe to trim his roses, polish his car, take the dog for a walk – a euphemism for violating by-laws on public hygiene, and a source of great complaint at those periodic gatherings where the police officially meet the community – and spy on his neighbours.

Review

What is the police product, and how does it relate to law and morality?

Do the police exist simply to enforce the law?

Clearly not. The police form part of the criminal justice system: but they are not there simply to enforce the law – as our sources acknowledge. Moreover, even the notion that the police are primarily a law-enforcement agency creates difficulties.

Which laws? The police cannot enforce all the laws all the time. They exercise discretion as to which laws to enforce and when to enforce them; and they have other methods of achieving or restoring order or rectifying injustice. Moreover, other agencies such as customs and excise also enforce laws.

If enforcing the law is a major purpose of the police, then they are not very successful in their task. The law forbids stealing, house-breaking and car theft. These are crimes which the police would like to stop. But they are very popular activities, and relatively safe for the criminal to pursue, in many areas. Detection rates vary considerably; but a large urban force that solves more than 30 per cent of reported crimes is doing reasonably well, judging by national statistics.

That's all very well: but improvement is possible, surely?

Of course it is. But although a police force may increase its efficiency considerably in investigating crime, there must come a point where the law of diminishing returns applies, and further improve-ments are more expensive than they are worth; or where crime is simply displaced elsewhere; or where the service realizes that since it cannot, except marginally, address the *causes* of crime, its effectiveness in resolving it must be limited.

Do the police exist to uphold morality?

Neither the 1962 Royal Commission nor the 1993 White Paper appears to mention morality. Nevertheless, some phrases have moral connotations. What is the need to protect, help and reassure the community, if not a moral aim? In a sense, everything that the police do is a moral activity: but if we try to frame their work in explicitly moral terms, we find problems.

Whose morality?

It is a contemporary platitude that we live in a heterogeneous society which does not retain the simple, clear, shared morality of the past. Opinion polls tend to show some agreement as to what people believe is wrong, but not as to how morality might be enforced: and opinion polls, as general election results indicate, are an uncertain guide to actual behaviour. It would be a bold person who claimed that as a nation we share a certain morality. Within the context of the family, there would probably be a general agreement that it is wrong to bring children up to lie, cheat and steal; but those prohibitions are too general, and too open to the exceptions of adult life, to give the police the basis to declare and enforce a common morality.

How does one uphold morality?

The police are empowered only to enforce the law; and the law and morality, although related, are not the same. Adultery is widely regarded as immoral, but it is not illegal. The police would be grossly exceeding their powers if they attempted to prevent adultery. In a country such as Saudi Arabia, where adultery is investigated, there are two significant differences. First, religion, law and morality are virtually co-terminous. What the Koran forbids is also against the law. Secondly, there is a special police unit, the religious police, to enforce the more specifically moral aspects of the law.

Public opinion may support a particular moral stance by the police, for example in preventing children from drinking alcohol by means which are not strictly supported by law. However, if those measures also make it more difficult for adults to drink, this happy moral consensus is not likely to last very long. The police recognize that the law is a blunt instrument and that their powers are rightly limited, and would very much like parents to play a greater role in controlling their errant, mischievous, and on occasion law-breaking children. However, this is easier said than done, and attempts to put an assumed moral consensus into practice have often failed.

The police as morality

We could rephrase our proposition, and say that the police embody or exemplify morality in themselves. Their existence serves to show that selfless devotion to the community is possible. They are our guardians to the chosen land. Although some senior police officers have rather implied this sort of thing in their windier moments, I think that most of us would rightly question its practicability. We do not need, even if it were possible to achieve it, a breed of moral exemplars. We need a body of men and women of reasonable behaviour, who recognize that the law applies to them as well as to others, and who enforce it appropriately and impartially against all offenders. If police officers themselves break the law, then this simply serves to show that they are human. If they consistently break the law and get away with it, then we have a problem. The credibility of a police force is a delicate growth, easily damaged or destroyed, and difficult to reseed in the mud of public mockery.

Other options

Other possibilities can be dealt with more rapidly. We might say that the police exist to serve the state, the government, or the community. While there is an element of truth in all of these propositions, none is sufficiently robust to stand alone. It is tempting but incomplete to conclude that the police themselves decide what they do. If we modify this to say that the police have an overarching purpose to maintain or restore public tranquillity, and that they will use the law, aspects of morality, and the more convenient parts of religion in a pragmatic way to secure that end, then we shall be, perhaps, not so very far from the truth.

How the police carry out their role is as important as what we, or they, define that role to be. The police, like any other sensible organization, wish to remain in existence and to be in charge of themselves, rather than come under the command of others. This means not that they must be loved – that would be rather too much to expect, want or need – but that their existence, and sufficient degree of autonomy to achieve reasonable objectives, is generally accepted by the public at large, and by the more influential decision-makers within our system of representative democracy.

In order to achieve that discretion – this is, I think, the third sense in which we have used the word, and possibly its most important – the police must balance competing interests and find the middle ground.

Quality of service means quality of life

The police are an honourable body of men and women whose existence and activities contribute to the quality of life in the United Kingdom. Their efforts can never be sufficient to ensure civilized existence. Civilization, and by that we mean a civilized existence for the many and not just for an elite, depends upon a successful reaction between a wide range of elements. Those elements include:

- [ ] a sufficiency of natural resources;
- [ ] a developed infrastructure;
- [ ] a sense of national identity and purpose;
- [ ] a reasonable level of education;
- [ ] a wide circulation of information;
- [ ] the practice and appreciation of cultural, sporting and leisure activities by a significant proportion of the population;
- [ ] the transmission of civilized values from one generation to another; and a range of other factors to which the police contribute directly in some cases, and indirectly in others.

What is clear is that the police do contribute, and that if we try to identify or limit their role or product too precisely, we are making a great mistake.

Constitutions may be drafted by constitutionalists, or evolve as the result of the interactions of men and women over time. The result, however, is not brought to life by constitutionalists, but by those who have to make ideals work in practice; and it is the actions of the people who work in the lower echelons of the public service which decide whether or not the ordinary citizen is treated with justice, compassion and humanity. We may judge a civilized nation by how it handles the power to coerce; and it is the police who have been given that power.

The *Statement of Common Purpose and Values*, put out by the Association of Chief Police Officers in 1991, is a fine exposition of what is needed:

> The purpose of the police service is to uphold the law fairly and firmly; to prevent crime; to pursue and bring to justice those who break the law; to keep the Queen's Peace; to protect, help, and reassure the community; and to be seen to do all this with integrity, common sense, and sound judgement.
>
> We must be compassionate, courteous and patient, acting without fear or favour or prejudice to the rights of others. We need to be professional, calm and restrained in the face of violence and apply only that force which is necessary to accomplish our lawful duty.
>
> We must strive to reduce the fears of the public and, so far as we can, reflect their priorities in the action we take. We must respond to well-founded criticism with a willingness to change.

Fine words. They cannot always be achieved; but their utterance is necessary.

CONCLUSION

I have laid out eight axioms about ethics, and gone on to analyse the role of the British police within the context of the values of liberal democracy. Our unwritten constitution is ambiguous about what the police stand for, and what they are supposed to do; and it is much easier to say what we do not want from the police, than what we do. What is clear is that the police do and must make moral judgements.

And now for the question I floated, but never addressed. Can one be a moral person in an immoral society? I had hoped to write a book on ethics without discussing the rather overworked example of Nazi Germany, but it fits here. The Nazis could and did project an ethical code which justified their activities, and the explicit acceptance of 'ethics' does not resolve all moral problems. Racial murderers and torturers can be consistent in their beliefs, and even a perverted ideology can be justified by its own logic. However, if we apply a full ethical analysis to any such ideology as National Socialism or Marxism-Leninism, it will fail. We may refer to the Word of God; Socratic Reason; the Roman concept of Natural Law; the Higher Common Sense, which Flora Poste mentioned with such approval in *Cold Comfort Farm*; or simply the Voice of Conscience. Something overrides ideology and there are some absolutes.

3

THE MORAL PRESSURES INVOLVED IN THE INVESTIGATION OF CRIME

The primary object of an efficient police is the prevention of crime; the next, that of the detection and apprehension of offenders when crime is committed. To these ends, all the efforts of the police must be directed.

Rowan and Mayne

Recruiting informants is the dirtiest aspect of police work. Everything else is theory. This is the reality. You do it any way you can.

Senior Lebanese police officer

Handling informants is the most difficult thing you can do.... It splits you right down the middle.'

Senior Indian police officer

I keep two sets of records. One is the list of my official informants. The other is the list of my private sources, whom I would never declare.... If I were asked to keep accounts, I would keep two sets of those as well.'

Senior Indian police officer

The most important thing in life is sincerity.... Once you've learned to fake that, you can achieve anything.

Attributed to the comedian Bob Monkhouse

INTRODUCTION

Like salt and pepper, crime and policing go together. As the first Commissioners of the Metropolitan Police pointed out, crime should ideally be prevented before it occurs. In practice, although measures designed to prevent crime may have some effect (but are impossible to measure, since we cannot prove *why* a crime has not occurred), the police need to devote a considerable part of their resources to the investigation of crime once it has occurred. However, we are still skirting round the issue; for in reality, the police may have knowledge of crime which has not yet occurred, but which is being planned. What should they do then? Prevent it? Disrupt it? Or allow the crime to occur, under controlled conditions which lead to a successful prosecution and the removal of dangerous criminals from the streets? These are both practical and moral dilemmas, exacerbated by the pressures of time, secrecy and the need for success.

Once the police begin to investigate crime actively, by using surveillance or informants to track crimes being contemplated, then major ethical dilemmas occur. Consider the following scenario, which demonstrates the problems of addressing crime when it is unclear whether you should prevent it happening, or allow it to begin and then intervene; and if the latter, when, how, and at what risk.

ACTIVITY

Setting the scene

You are the head of CID for a quiet country area, and receive information that a bank robbery is being planned.

The source is a female informant who has been cultivated by one of your most experienced detectives over a long period of time. You have only recently learned her identity, and have never met her. Her information comes to you second-hand, via Detective Constable Johnston. Johnston is an old-fashioned detective who believes in playing things very close to his chest, and puts little or nothing down on paper, and you have had to spend some time gaining his confidence. Since no records have been kept you cannot objectively grade his source, and all you know is that in his opinion she is reliable. What follows is written from his perspective, from the notes you made in conversation with him.

The robbery will take place, your source thinks, on the next Friday afternoon; but she is not quite sure of the time.

The target is the bank in the busy High Street of your local market town.

Three to four men will take part.

They will be armed with sawn-off shotguns and a Kalashnikov automatic rifle. She is not sure whether or not they have any ammunition to go with the rifle, which was bought on the black market and may be more of a status symbol in the criminal fraternity than something they intend to use.

The men will wear masks to carry out the robbery, and make their getaway in a car parked nearby which has yet to be stolen. She does not know the identity of the car thief and getaway driver. From what she has overheard being discussed, the gang intend to use someone who has no criminal record.

Finally, your source has given this information because she is the older sister of the leader of the gang and purchaser of the Kalashnikov. Jim is a dyed-in-the-wool criminal, as she admits, but has never done anything like this before.

Mary is giving you this information very reluctantly, because she thinks that her brother and his friends have gone crazy and are totally out of their depth. She wants your promise that no harm will come to Jim. She does not want her own identity revealed under any circumstances.

In this situation, what would you do?

Standard operating procedures

Every force has guidelines advising you what to do in this sort of situation. Let us assume that yours do not help you in this case. You are on your own.

Home Office guidelines

There are Home Office guidelines on the use of informants, which for example prescribe the use of *agents provocateur*. We shall come to those later. Let us assume for the moment that this is a test of your judgement from first principles, and not of your interpretation of the relevant guidelines.

The law

Clearly, police officers should not break the law; and clearly, the law proscribes certain activities, such as taking part in a criminal conspiracy. Let us suppose that you have no access to any case law which would indicate to you what the courts have found acceptable or unacceptable in the past.

Options

1. Do nothing

To do nothing would be professionally, ethically and criminally irresponsible.

2. Find out more

Certainly, and about everything; but let us suppose that you still face a dilemma. You do not and will never have perfect information. Nor would perfect information give you a plan. Even if you can find out more about criminal plans, weaponry, transport, personnel and tactics, you still have to weigh it all up and make a decision as to what to do.

3. Set up a proper system for registering and controlling informants

Certainly; but that does not solve this problem.

4. Seek advice

Yes; but advice is not a decision. A strategy still needs to be chosen.

5. Prevent the crime occurring, by deterrence or disruption

a. Increasing patrols

If you simply increase patrols in the area of the bank, you may deter the gang from robbing it that Friday; but they could return on another day, when you are no longer patrolling in such strength. On the other hand, if they are tooled and psyched up and looking for action, they may rob another bank that same day, which they had not previously selected and which you could not know about. If they have not planned and made a reconnaissance in regard to the alternative robbery, then things are even more likely to go wrong.

'Not my responsibility', did I hear you say? It certainly is. We all have a duty to prevent crime if we can, and as a police officer you carry an additional and specific burden of responsibility.

b. Warning the bank staff of what may happen

You may do this because you feel that it is your duty to warn people of a threat, whatever your plan for dealing with the robbers. Or you may feel that if you warn the bank staff they will be able to prevent the robbery themselves, either by increasing visible security at the bank, or by letting it be generally known that their security arrangements over money are such that it would be impossible for the staff to give a large sum to any robber, not matter what threats were made.

If you increase security at the bank, you face the problem that the robbers may turn their attentions elsewhere and carry out a plan of which you have no current knowledge. Moreover, you may be less likely to gain that knowledge than before, because you cannot be sure what the bank will do with the information you give them. The gang could suspect a leak, and from then on discuss their plans where your informant cannot hear them.

Detective Constable Johnston will not like you to spread his information any further than is absolutely necessary, because he will suppose that his source will be threatened with exposure. Clearly, there are times when a source must be exposed: but is this occasion one of them?

6. Arrest the gang now

You have the basis for making an arrest here, in that you believe that three or four men are planning an armed robbery and are already in possession of illegally-held or modified firearms. However, you have no case against them if your informant is unwilling or unsuited to give evidence. If you arrest them and search the premises, you may not find the weapons, and you will have given your hand away.

7. Arrest the gang on the way to the bank, with their weapons

This is a high risk/high gain strategy. First, you need to be sure that you can remain in contact with the gang, and can plan where to prepare and spring an effective ambush. Secondly, you are risking an armed confrontation, in which the public, the police and the criminals themselves may be injured or killed. You may not be too worried about what happens to the criminals – although even that is an area for moral debate. But you do have to ask yourself: is the risk justified? Do you really control the situation to the extent that you could describe your plan as reasonable?

8. Arrest the gang at the bank

This poses the same risks as 7, with a greater likelihood of injury to innocent bystanders. The cry: 'Stop! Armed police!' may lead to the robbers surrendering, their hands in the air. Or they may open fire, or take hostages.

9. Arrest the gang afterwards

You may have lessened the risk of armed confrontation at the bank. However, you are still taking the risk that something could go wrong and someone be killed or injured. Moreover, you are allowing a serious crime to occur. The police exist to prevent or deter crime. This achieves neither. In addition, the gang may escape altogether, or destroy the evidence of their crime, or otherwise muddy a good case against them.

10. Allow the robbery to take place without interference of any kind. Gather evidence passively, for future prosecution

You are still taking the risk that something could go wrong and someone be killed or injured. Moreover, you are allowing a serious crime to occur, and possibly committing a criminal offence yourself. The police exist to prevent or deter crime. This achieves neither.

Commentary

Depending on the circumstances, a number of these options could be justified as being of greater or lesser appropriateness. It is important to recognize the following points:

- [ ] No option is likely to prove perfect.
- [ ] The decision maker should seek as much advice as possible.
- [ ] The inevitable area of uncertainty should be reduced as much as possible before any plan is made.
- [ ] The plan adopted should be defendable under force policy, with a written explanation in support.

Policy lays down priorities. For example, in the case of armed robbery, it would be important:

1. To act within the law.
2. To preserve public safety.
3. To prevent crime, if possible.
4. If it occurs, to arrest its perpetrators, if possible.
5. To protect the source of your information, if possible.

These priorities might be taken to indicate that the best option, if you have knowledge that a bank robbery is going to occur, is to use your information to stop it happening by deterrence or disruption. However, other interpretations are possible. For example, you might argue that in a particular case it would be an acceptable risk to allow the robbers to put their weapons in a car and set off towards the bank, only to be safely arrested according to a prearranged strategy. They would then be arrested red-handed, receive lengthy jail sentences, and cease to be a public menace for some time. In any discussion of the options, two or more heads would obviously be better than one, provided that the security of the information could be maintained.

THE CRIMINAL PROCESS

In this chapter we shall look at the ethical problems that arise in the handling of crime, before, while and after it is carried out. We shall have much to say about specialist investigators such as CID, but we shall also be discussing the overall way in which the police are organized to combat crime. Why? Because this book is about better decision making in a strategic sense, as well as a tactical one. If an interrogator attacks a prisoner, that is bad behaviour. But was the interrogation necessary in the first place? Could the crime have been prevented by better strategy in planning and use of resources? And if the interrogation were necessary, should not its possible breakdown have been anticipated, and guarded against as far as were reasonable?

CRIME PREVENTION

Arguably, if the police devote a sufficient proportion of their resources to the prevention of crime, then they will have less need to investigate it, for there will be less crime committed. Although the new police began as a crime prevention agency, and no separate CID was created until 1842, investigating crime soon became rather more popular than preventing it. In a modern police force the crime prevention department is likely to be small, under-funded, and of inferior status to CID. Crime prevention is typically associated with offering advice on bolts and window-locks; CID with chasing villains in fast cars. Which would you rather do?

While in theory any patrolling police constable may discourage crime simply by walking his beat, in practice this is not relied upon as an effective or very scientific means of crime prevention, and where police constables still walk the beat (an increasingly rare phenomenon) they are there to reassure the public, or gain local knowledge, rather than to prevent crime directly.

Ethics is about good decision making, and the allocation of resources is an area where good decisions need to be made. Many police officers who work in crime prevention still feel that they are the Cinderellas of the police service.

If the fundamental purpose of the police is to reduce crime, then the seriousness with which a chief constable investigates the effectiveness of crime prevention policies, and the proportion of his resources which he accordingly allocates to crime prevention, is a measure of his capacity to make responsible and effective decisions.

INFORMANTS

It is as easy to deceive ourselves without noticing as it is hard to deceive others without their noticing.

The cleverest subtlety of all is knowing how to appear to fall into traps set for us; people are never caught so easily as when they set out to catch others.

Maxims, Duc de la Rochefoucauld

Whatever the emphasis upon crime prevention, some crimes will still be planned and committed; and those crimes will need to be investigated. Informants may be used at any stage of the process of investigating crime. I shall concentrate upon the ethical dilemmas which occur to do with informants, particularly in those cases when informants provide information before a crime has been committed. You have already addressed this as an activity to do with bank-robbery. Let us now go into greater detail.

Presuppositions

1. Police services need to use informants to be effective in investigating crime.
2. The British police service is actively committed to the use of informants in its campaign against crime, and this trend is likely to continue.
3. The use of informants raises inescapable moral dilemmas.
4. The police service recognizes this, and issues guidelines from time to time as to how informers should be recruited, trained and controlled. The purpose of these guidelines is, *inter alia*, to prevent dilemmas arising, and to suggest ways of resolving them should they arise notwithstanding. As is the way of the world, guidelines often concern themselves with procedure.
5. These instructions cannot provide a complete answer in what is and will remain an immensely difficult area of police operations.
6. It is desirable that the police continue to cultivate and use informers, and that further help is provided to enable them to gain or improve their skills in this area.

Problems with handling informants

As we know, the police service has traditionally operated as a craft in which decisions are made by operators without consulting others, on the basis of their own judgement. Imagine, for a moment, that the opposite applied:

> '*I think I understand the position now, Detective Constable. You're offering to waive a prosecution for a motoring offence, if your source tells you when the next armed robbery is to take place.*'
> 'That's it ... Sir.'
> '*I see. And what is the logic behind your calculation?*'
> 'I beg your pardon?'
> '*How do you compare the two offences? Do you award them points on a scale of evil, or what?*'

'Well, I suppose so, Sir. I hadn't really thought about it. Obviously an armed robbery is a more serious crime than a motoring offence – or at any rate, this motoring offence. We know that from the penalty which the law imposes.'

'*Good point. Go on.*'

'Harry is a good source. He's never let me down. There are a lot of crimes which would never have been solved without him. After all, we are here to solve crimes, aren't we, Sir? And how can we do it, if we don't have any information?'

'*I take your point, Detective Constable. And now I'm going to ask you a very difficult question.*'

'Go on, Sir.'

'*How does Harry know about these robberies?*'

'He mixes with the wrong sort of people, Sir.'

'*You mean criminals.*'

'That's right, Sir. Otherwise he wouldn't know anything, would he?'

'*Quite. Does he have form?*'

'Oh, Lord yes, Sir. He's got quite a record, has our Harry. He's a right villain.'

'*So ... let me get this right. You are proposing to use as an informant*' ...

'Beg pardon, Sir. Already using.'

'*You are already using as an informant, a known and convicted criminal.*'

'That's right, Sir.'

'*Who knows a good deal about armed robberies.*'

'Yes.'

'*Because he takes part in them himself.*'

'I wouldn't know that, Sir. I never asked him.'

Abstract? Fanciful? Ridiculous? Clearly, the dialogue is unreal, but the dilemma is not. If the police service is to combat crime effectively, it must use informers; and those informers are unlikely to be of much use unless they are close to the perpetration of crimes.

Problems with informants – Issues

☐ The role of the supervisor.

☐ The relationship between informant and handler.

☐ The value of the information offered, compared with the value of what is given in exchange.

☐ The process of converting information or criminal intelligence into evidence that can be used in court.

☐ There is also the overall problem as to how the police use of informants affects their general relationship with the public. After all, if the police are attempting to convey an image of decency and wholesomeness, the cultivation of informants is hard to reconcile with this. People know that the police have to fight crime: but need that mean getting into the bear-pit with the criminals?

Not all the things that might go wrong in this dynamic and volatile area do so, and there is a great deal that experienced and level-headed police officers can do to avoid the more obvious mistakes of informant handling. However, if we make the assumption that *all* police officers, at least potentially, are informant handlers, and should be encouraged to develop and exploit sources as far as possible, then this multiplies the possible number of mistakes that can be made. Most informers are recruited when already in police custody; and most interviews are carried out, not by dedicated and highly experienced detectives, but by ordinary working constables who usually have no special expertise in this area.

Research

Openly available research on the effectiveness of the use of informants is hard to find, for obvious reasons. One recent study is a paper presented at the Academy of Criminal Justice Sciences Conference, Boston, USA, in March 1995, by Colin Dunningham, entitled 'The Role of the Police Informer in the British Criminal Justice System'.

> Recent years have seen British police forces placing increasing emphasis upon the more proactive use of intelligence resources.... Drawing on the findings of a two year project, the paper questions the widely held belief of senior officers that informers are an efficient, cost-effective resource and identifies negative consequences that informer-based policing policies are producing for individual police officers, police forces, and ultimately the criminal justice system.

Dunningham's analysis is based on a wide-ranging piece of research, during which he examined 114 cases involving the use of informers, interviewed in depth 62 police officers and 11 professional informers, and read 198 questionnaires. Among the negative consequences he identified are that police officers are being encouraged to cultivate informers when they have neither the training nor the experience to do so properly. Moreover, they lack confidence in the ability or willingness of their senior officers to carry out an effective supervisory role.

Nearly three quarters of all detectives who responded to the questionnaire thought that you could not be sure of general supervisory support when things went wrong.... Half of the senior officers in our sample also thought that supervisors were out of touch with the reality of running informers and unsupportive when things went wrong.

Only one in three detectives would ask for advice from their informer controller if they had a problem with running a registered informer. The majority would ask either another constable or their sergeant for advice.

Dunningham's research, which is supported by anecdotal evidence, suggests that many police managers do not know enough about informant handling to be of much practical help in this area. This problem has been exacerbated by the fact that officers with little experience in CID are now being promoted to positions of authority therein, on the theory that:

☐ management is management, whatever the product or service;
☐ it is necessary for their career development; and
☐ there are advantages to breaking up the traditional culture of CID by bringing in relative outsiders to question established practices.

All three of these reasons may be valid on their own terms. However, their impact is unlikely to improve the quality of expert supervision. Dunningham suggests that in many cases the information that the informer has to offer is not worth the reward he expects in return. Often, the reward is that the law be expected to turn a blind eye to what is supposedly a lesser offence, in order that a greater offence be cleared up. However, it is not always obvious which is the lesser offence; it does not always follow that the reward offered is necessary; and it is certainly far from clear that the whole process is properly managed. The calculation as to what should be done is often made by a junior officer, without much experience of informant handling, who is likely to be both more enthusiastic and gullible than a more experienced bargainer.

Dunningham quotes one detective saying in relation to an informer of his:

He does a lot of driving without documents and I help him out every couple of months or so with that.

However, in the sixteen months that this officer had run this informer, only three pieces of minor intelligence had been received from him and only one arrest, for a minor offence of burglary at commercial premises, had resulted....

A detective sergeant, in defending the non-prosecution of informers for minor traffic related offences said:

'A lot of (uniformed officers) understand, but many don't. Because of their sub-culture they don't understand that a dwelling-house burglary is worth more than 20 vehicle defects. I think the courts are partly to blame for this. They fine somebody £200 for a dwelling-house burglary, but £400 for the traffic offences....

Of course a traffic officer would say that the guy with a defective vehicle may kill somebody while a dwelling-house burglary only breaks someone's heart.'

The traffic officer may be saying something of great value! There are a range of motoring offences which could be used to bargain with an informant. Many of us might agree that the full majesty of the law need not be invoked if someone parks illegally, and that parking tickets are fair game for bargaining purposes. It could be argued that someone who is driving with defective tyres or other faults to his vehicle need not necessarily be prosecuted. After all, the offender could be told that the offence will not be prosecuted this time, but that he must put things right. But what about where it comes to driving without insurance, or driving while under the influence of alcohol? Surely some offences are so careless of the common good that they simply must be prosecuted – whatever might be gained if they were not? And in any case, what is to be the effect on other officers, and on the public at large, if certain people are seen to be above the law? In a calm and objective Radio 4 programme that investigated the whole question of the use of informants, broadcast in October 1996, it was pointed out that since informants are often unreliable, manipulative and dangerous, this is an area of police work which must cause difficulties; and those difficulties are not confined to spectacular mistakes, such as have arisen, for example, in the use of informants to penetrate and inform the police upon criminal activities within ethnic minorities.

The way forward

We cannot decide upon a policy by considering a single case or issue, but by identifying what are the relevant factors and making the decision in the light of their comparative importance. We must acknowledge that handlers will never be satisfied with what an informant apparently knows at a particular time. Informant handling is a dynamic process and the handler is always be going to be pressing for further information. That, however, increases rather than removes the need to analyse the situation as it is understood at time x, and make a decision.

The potential benefits of what is on offer are relatively easily calculated. The risks need to be spelled out in terms of their nature, likelihood and severity. They may be sub-categorized as practical, legal and ethical, although in practice the three will overlap. Having dissected and analysed the problem, weighing up both options and risks, we will be in a better position to make a considered and defendable decision. We explore this process further in our chapter on decision making as a process.

Conclusion

Real police work is not a matter of clear, absolute moral standards being leisurely applied in easily grasped situations. It means incomplete information, competing priorities and rapid decisions. Its pressures have been used as an argument to defend a rule-of-thumb method of decision making which is indefensible. Logical, systematic, and recorded decision making to an agreed policy need not take long: but it must occur.

UNDERCOVER OPERATIONS

One of the more difficult tasks which may face members of the service is how to evaluate someone's ability to work undercover as a means of investigating crime. Working undercover ranges from temporarily concealing one's identity as a servant of the crown, to a situation in which the police officer sets out to infiltrate a criminal, terrorist or otherwise illegal organization by posing as a member, potential recruit, or active sympathizer. We shall talk about undercover work at three levels:

1. Casual work.
2. Sustained activity.
3. Professional agentry.

Level 3 is not our concern. This is specialized work, carried out by very specialized people, of whom as members of the general public we may read only very occasionally, although there is a great deal about them in fiction. To infiltrate an active terrorist organization such as the IRA is exceedingly difficult and dangerous, not least because that organization is extraordinarily security conscious, and has the natural advantage that almost all of its active members and sympathizers come from a very small, close-knit community of a few hundred families – what the army used to used to call 'Eton and Sandhurst IRA'. The IRA's recruiting ground is limited to a select area within the small province of Northern Ireland. Its recruits are united by background, religion, indoctrination, habits, accent, and use of English. And the possibility of a member of the security forces infiltrating such an organization is exceedingly remote. (For a vivid depiction of the difficulties which will arise if you do attempt such a feat, I recommend the excellent novel *Harry's Game*, by Gerald Seymour.) There are moral dilemmas aplenty at level 3, but we need not suppose that the active police officer, who is the typical reader of this book, is likely to work in this area.

Level 1

We might call this 'casual deception'. Every police force practises this from time to time, and it is part of the tradecraft of an experienced sergeant or inspector to be able to manage the process.

> Harry ... I've got a little job for you tonight. Won't take long. Get changed into civvies, will you?

Harry is being asked to go and check out a cafe where stolen cigarettes are reported to be sold, to see what he can find out and report back. He is to practise deception, in that he is not to reveal that he is a police officer. If possible, he should avoid the issue. But he has not been given a cover story. No elaborate deception plan is being prepared. This is a casual act of deception, which is unlikely to cause any great problems, and of which any competent police unit will be capable. Let us move on to the next level.

Level 2

This is the level at which a police officer is expected to carry out a sustained act of deception, which will involve preparation, dedication and skill. Let us suppose, for example, that the police need to know what is going on inside a gang of football hooligans. No football hooligan is offering himself as an informant, and the police are stuck for current information. In this situation, it is easy to understand the attraction of the idea of using a police officer to infiltrate a gang. After all, the gang is not, as far as is known, seriously criminal. The officer will not be placed at great risk. He will not have to learn an elaborate cover story. He will only have to know a great deal about football, which many police officers will already. He need not stay underground very long. He will be expected to have a life outside football, and need not be with the gang all the time.

Problems with undercover work

1. Selection

Psst .... Want to do something special?

The person who volunteers for this sort of work may not be the person who is best suited to it. Other methods of selection are difficult – undercover work is not usually advertised in force orders – although it is possible to raise standards by national agreement and professional selection procedures.

2. Coping

Just make sure no one asks you to shoot anybody. All right?

Any undercover work can give problems, practical, ethical and legal, and these become more difficult as one approaches level 2. Work of this sort may be very much more difficult than at first appears. The potential pressures are considerable. The infiltrator is being asked to build up a quick and convincing rapport with a group of people who may be lawless in the conventional sense, but who will have a very strong sense of group identity and a very clear set of rules as to what is and is not acceptable behaviour. In order for the infiltrator to be accepted, he will need to understand and be able to live by their code. That will mean not just passive compliance but active enthusiasm. If the infiltrator is to show active enthusiasm, he will have to live the part. The longer that the role is sustained, the greater the problems that may occur. In addition, the undercover operator may have to make quick, difficult decisions as to what he should or should not do, without benefit of advice.

3. The aftermath

I don't care what you've just been doing. You're in uniform now!

Before the operation starts, thought should be given to what will happen afterwards. What sort of debriefing will the infiltrator receive? Will he be expected to testify in court? Will he expect to return to normal duties immediately? Will he have developed a taste for deception? The organization may not have a legal obligation to care for its operators, but it has a moral one. (Under the notion of a duty of care, the police service has a legal obligation to reduce or ameliorate stress.)

Altogether, work of this sort needs very careful planning if it is not to go wrong. From the ethical point of view, one of the main considerations is one of fairness.

Is it fair to exploit someone who enjoys this sort of work and repeatedly volunteers for it – even though it may not be in his long-term interests? Is it fair to use someone who is not obviously suitable in personality, but whose background is right for a particular deception? How do we engage his services, and how much pressure is involved? Where does the responsibility of the organization stop, and that of the individual begin?

ACTIVITY

You work as a shift inspector in a busy part of a large city which has a major problem with drugs. Many of the drugs transactions are taking place between black people, and it is very difficult for a predominantly white police force to find out the information they need. The local black people do not talk very much to the police, whether through antipathy or fear, and surveillance is almost impossible.

A black constable is posted to your area. He is young, keen and well-educated, and has no connections with the local neighbourhood. The head of the drugs squad learns of his arrival and immediately comes to see you. She wants to put the new constable out on the street in plain clothes, so that he can find out as much as he can about local drugs-dealing before it becomes known that he is a police officer. Before she approaches him, she wants to speak to you. What do you think of the scheme?

☐ What is your reaction to your colleague's suggestion?
☐ What difficulties could you see arising?
☐ What are the ethical aspects of this case, if any?

Commentary

Your reaction

Your reaction in a real situation would include your detailed knowledge of the local drugs problem, your awareness of measures which had been taken in the past to address it, your opinion of your colleague's integrity and professionalism, and other factors which cannot be simulated here. However, you will have had an overall reaction: perhaps, that this is not such a simple task as your colleague envisages.

Difficulties, practical and ethical

Choice

There is clearly an issue here about choice. Suppose the task is put to the black constable as voluntary. Will it be seen as such? After all, he is new, and presumably keen to make a good impression. Is he really going to say no, even if he feels disinclined?

Exploitation

Are you exploiting this officer's background, simply because it serves the organization's immediate purposes? Did he join the service to help its surveillance programme, or because he wanted to be a police officer? It would be easy to suggest to him that his cooperation will be greatly valued, that it could count in his favour, that this is the best way he can help the service, that it is all in a day's work, and so on. Are those statements really true?

Consequences

Will this officer be able to resume normal duties, if it is known that he has taken part in a deception plan?

Conclusion

It is not my intention in writing this book to stop all covert police operations! Provided that operations are necessary, carefully planned and managed, and use only properly selected volunteers, then the police service may benefit considerably from them. Life requires that we make choices. People are entitled to take reasonable risks for probable gains. Informed candidates will be able to evaluate for themselves the pressures and consequences of sustained deception. Uninformed candidates cannot do so. The decision maker needs to realize that what may have seemed purely a practical problem has an ethical dimension. Conversely, ethical issues cannot be solved by the application of moral philosophy alone. They require practical analysis.

ETHICAL DECISION MAKING, SOURCE HANDLING AND THE PRINCIPLES OF INTELLIGENCE

If no system is in place then isolated good practice can occur, but it is likely to be lost in a Sargasso Sea of conflicting currents and once-known passages. If the right system is in place, then source, handler and manager will find their places and roles within it. To design an efficient, effective and ethical intelligence system from scratch would be an enormous undertaking. Luckily, much of the work has already been done for us, in that the key principles on which intelligence work are best based are already known.

Principles of intelligence

The nine basic principles of intelligence work are as follows:

1. Centralized control

Intelligence work is like a huge jigsaw puzzle being completed by a large number of people working simultaneously in small groups. Each group has started in a different sector of the puzzle. Each has a number of pieces. Some groups may not have the appropriate pieces for their

. . . .

sector. No group has a picture of the completed puzzle. This situation requires centralized control.

2. Timeliness

An intelligence system is not an art form. It is not designed to be admired, but to be of use. We need to know about the impending bank robbery before it occurs.

3. Systematic exploitation

Sources and agencies should be used systematically, by methodical tasking.

4. Objectivity

As information flows in and the intelligence picture grows it is possible to become wedded to particular perceptions. It is essential to remain objective, giving fresh information its proper weight and not distorting it to fit preconceived ideas.

5. Accessibility

Relevant material must be available to intelligence staff and users, within the limits of security.

6. Responsiveness

Bureaucracies tend to be slow to change. An intelligence system must be capable of being responsive to new developments and demands.

7. Source protection

Sources of any kind must be adequately protected.

8. Continuous review

Intelligence must be constantly reviewed, taking into account all new information.

9. Security

Security is of the essence in intelligence work. Perhaps the most important aspect of security is the protection of sources. However, security is also necessary for a number of other reasons, including preventing leaks which could lead to operations being frustrated and sources being fed false information.

It will normally be appropriate to operate under a 'need to know' policy, and not a 'right to know'. Within the intelligence community there is likely to be a need for some subjects to be confined to very small groups, and for intelligence supplied to users to be sanitized. Clear and stringent security rules will be required.

But what about morality?

None of the traditional principles of intelligence mentions morality, or even legality. Intelligence is traditionally seen as an amoral activity, in which it is axiomatic that the end may be quoted to justify the means. Moreover, the practice or means itself is corrupting. In what other trade, occupation or profession are people trained and encouraged to lie, not only to those whom they are entitled to deceive, as it were, but to their colleagues, friends and family? Moral behaviour needs to be not only discussed but practised, said Aristotle, for it to become habitual; and intelligence work habituates one to immoral behaviour.

Peace and war

Military intelligence sees the law simply as a possible asset, to be used when it will further one's aims, and otherwise ignored. In wartime, different norms apply. Thus, in the early part of the second world war British intelligence officers were successful in capturing several German would-be spies, while their German handlers remained in ignorance of this. The German agents were then given a simple choice: work for us, or be shot as spies. One or two were shot; the others began to work for the British. They continued to do so, happily enough, for the rest of the war, during the course of which further would-be spies were sent to England – to be offered the same choice as the first arrivals. The story is described without moral comment in H C Masterman's *The Double Cross System of the War from 1939 to 1945*.

Lest it be assumed that this was an absolute British triumph, we must acknowledge that the Abwehr (German Military Intelligence) played precisely the same trick upon the agents we attempted to place in Holland: and we committed the same mistakes as the Germans, in failing to see the signs that our agents were not operating independently, but under duress. For the German account, see *London Calling North Pole*, author unknown.

In war we are prepared to allow the state to carry out extraordinary acts. In addition to double-crossing, consider the many tricks, ploys and stratagems described by Michael Howard in his history of strategic deception in the second world war (Howard, 1990). Some of these tricks were simply ingenious, rather than of questionable morality. For example, British Intelligence allowed a dead man to be washed ashore in occupied Europe with significant papers in his pocket, in an attempt to mislead the Nazis as to the location of the allied invasion of Europe. Was that immoral? Hardly. The British were perfectly entitled to deceive the enemy and save lives in doing so.

Indeed, we could take the argument further. The stakes were such that extreme measures might be justified on both utilitarian and absolutist grounds. The body used to deceive the Nazis was that of a man who had died of natural causes. Suppose we had had to kill someone to provide the body. What would have been one life sacrificed, against the tens of thousands of lives of allied soldiers which would be saved? Were not the Nazis so evil, that almost any means could be justified to bring their regime to an end?

What is acceptable – or open to consideration – in wartime, is a poor precedent for peace; and the police would be ill-advised to take war as their template for deception and other ploys. Power corrupts, said Lord Acton: and whatever is secret decays. Intelligence work combines both power and secrecy. Rather than attempt to prevent corruption and decay by moral exhortation, challenging group norms, providing counselling, or other measures of doubtful efficacy, why not use management techniques established and tested in other areas? There is no reason why the normal canons and practices of good management should not be applied within an overall context which recognizes that some information, and the method by which it was acquired, must be kept secret. If your system allows for source handlers to claim expenses for paying informants who do not in fact exist; if it does not set out to verify or falsify their information, having established that it was not simply invented by the handler in the first place; and if it allows the intelligence operative a latitude in what he does, which would not be allowed in any other form of police work; then your system is in need of reform: not because it is being exploited, but because it might be. It is simply bad practice.

System

Before you can put in measures to check procedures, you must have established some recognizable procedures in the first place. That is why an established system for gathering and using intelligence, based upon the nine principles we have already enunciated, is a good foundation for further work in making the system ethical.

Am I avoiding the real ethical issues, by suggesting the use of general management techniques in this area? I think not. It is perfectly ethical to prevent a potential problem arising, and it does not indicate a lack of trust. Would a bank teller say he was not trusted, because it were established practice in a bank that every financial transaction be checked by someone else? The system does not indicate that he personally is under suspicion. It recognizes the possibility of mistakes. He would accept it as normal practice, and be pleased that he alone does not bear the responsibility for what he does.

INTERROGATION

In order to be able to do their work, police officers need to be able to interrogate people. 'Interrogate' is a loaded word, and 'interview' is now the preferred term.

Whom do the police question? In three words: victims, witnesses and suspects. These categorizations are not exclusive. A victim or a witness may also be a suspect, and a suspect may also be a victim in a series of incidents. Most of what follows will be primarily concerned with the ethics of how the police question suspects. However, what we shall say can be applied to the ethics of all police interviews.

Before I start, a word of caution. If you ask a police officer whether or not the rules that govern questioning are ever broken, you may be told:

- [ ] that this never happens; *or*
- [ ] that the rules may be 'bent' occasionally. The word 'bent' is so much more satisfying than 'broken'. 'Broken' is so stark; so simplistic; so undiscretionary; *or*
- [ ] that the rules used to be broken: but that was all long ago. Why, the raconteur remembers that when he started policing....

In reality, most of us break rules sometimes: and why should police officers be any different? I shall proceed on the assumption that any police officer, British or otherwise, will have an interest in reading this section which is more than simply academic. Secondly, I shall assume that most police officers could quite easily put forward an argument against rule-breaking in this area, if asked to do so; and that such an argument would be phrased in moral terms of universal human rights, unintended consequences, and sympathetic imagination. Thus:

> What if I were arrested (quite by accident, of course) and found myself being interrogated? Would I be so sure that the police always catch the right people, so that it doesn't really matter what they do to them? Or would I suddenly feel rather differently, about the need for a police moral code?
>
> What if the person being interrogated were my daughter? Would I still accept the same arguments then, about the need for the use of judicious stimulation?
>
> Where do we stop? If we allow violence to be used against (say) a terrorist, a hardened criminal, a recalcitrant pervert, will we not end by using it against anyone?

However, the theoretical argument that most police officers could construct against the abuse of power does not mean that power has never been abused.

Traditional police interrogation methods were at best rough and ready, and at worst casually brutal. Although in law a man is innocent until proved guilty, that assumption did not hold ground in the interrogation room, where a variety of techniques would be used to attempt to make the suspect confess to the crime – the assumption being, presumably, that if he held out against all of them, one should look somewhere else. Methods included:

- [ ] harsh questioning;
- [ ] casual violence;
- [ ] deprivation of sleep, rest and refreshment;
- [ ] lying and other forms of deception;
- [ ] psychological tricks, such as confrontation;
- [ ] blackmail (as the word is commonly used, rather than in its legal definition);
- [ ] bargaining and pseudo-bargaining;
- [ ] the establishment of moral superiority, leading to a psychological dependence in which the suspect felt an over-whelming urge to confess;
- [ ] in extreme cases, a confession would simply be fabricated.

Any of these methods might be used on its own, or in combination with others. Experienced interrogators realized the usefulness of blending techniques, for example by following a harsh questioner with a soft one, whose apparent approachability might encourage the suspect to lower his defences. However, not many police interrogators were broadly experienced. Learning was purely from doing, and there was no attempt made to pass on technique in a systematic and structured way.

To understand what could go wrong in an interview, either deliberately or accidentally, look at the range of provisions of PACE, the Police and Criminal Evidence Act of 1984, which exists to prevent abuses of investigation. PACE sets out provisions to protect any prisoner from ill-treatment or abuse, and then specifies particular measures to protect people especially prone to danger, such as the blind, the deaf, the dumb, the mentally or physically ill, the juvenile, the sub-normal, and the non-English speaking. Justice must be both fair and seen to be fair, and in these cases it is right that the unequal be treated unequally. The concept of fairness, as Aristotle pointed out, does not mean that everyone should be treated as the same.

Among those whom PACE was designed to protect were the people who in the past were convicted of crimes which they did not commit, on the basis of a false confession. The phenomenon of false confession (Gudjonsson, 1992) is not confined to the British system, but is universal. The French police do not have PACE: they have an equivalent set of rules for police procedure. In August 1996 a Cornish schoolgirl on holiday with her friends in France was raped and murdered in a hostel, and the French police have yet (at the time of writing) to catch the murderer. They thought that they had him – a likely suspect, of known criminal record and no fixed address, was picked up and questioned, and confessed to the crime quite quickly – but DNA tests showed that he could not have been the rapist, and he was eliminated from the inquiry. This case supports Gisli Gudjonsson's assertion that false confessions have often been made, and demonstrates the dangers of relying upon the confession as sole evidence of guilt, whether or not the techniques used to obtain it are over-zealous.

Effective and ethical interviewing

The matrix of techniques available to the police interviewer falls into four categories:

- [ ] Moral and effective.
- [ ] Immoral and effective.
- [ ] Moral but ineffective.
- [ ] Immoral and ineffective.

Immoral and ineffective techniques

Some of the techniques which we listed initially can be criticized as being both immoral and ineffective. Casual violence, for example, comes into the same category as the brutal, inhuman or degrading conduct which is outlawed under the Universal Declaration of Human Rights. It is bound to have a brutalizing effect upon the perpetrator and his assistants; it will bring the organization as a whole into disrepute; and it may well lead to false confessions. By the time you are really feeling under pressure, you will tell the interrogator what you think he wants to hear.

Other techniques

Can interviewing be both ethical and effective? The consensus of opinion is that it can. A proper interview is a well-prepared, systematic and logical exploration of the facts, which is intended to uncover the truth. No police interrogation which relies upon immoral techniques can be effective, in the real sense of the word: for it weakens the integrity of the criminal justice system of which it is a part. If someone cannot be interrogated effectively under the present rules, it is wrong to break them. If a hardened criminal or terrorist will not respond to a normal interview, then other ways must be used to pursue justice against that person, from the range of techniques which are legally and morally acceptable.

Deception by lying

Deception has many forms. One is lying: ie, deliberately stating as true something that you know to be false, or have no proof is true. A favourite interrogation technique, as used by many interviewers (and not just in the context of police work) is to lie and note the reaction. Is a police officer entitled to lie to a prisoner, in order to find out the truth? Suppose this script:

Officer: 'Did you do it?'
Suspect: 'No.'

> *Officer:* '*That's not what your friend says.*'
> Suspect: 'What's he been saying, then?'
> *Officer:* '*He said you stole the car.*' (This was never said.)
> Suspect: 'That's a lie! He did it!'

There are infinite variations on this little pastiche, which is offered simply as an illustration of a lie. In some cases, the police would have confronted the two suspects, each believing that the other had already incriminated him. The line between policework and drama is sometimes hard to draw.

Is this lie justified? Are we entitled to lie to a suspected criminal, in the hope of inducing him to incriminate himself or others? My analysis will be based on ethical principles rather than legal precedent or interpretation of PACE, and does not relate specifically to any unsafe convictions that may have occurred – although the reader is entitled to apply the logic expressed here to such cases.

Arguments in favour of deception by lying

1. An innocent person has nothing to fear.
2. A conviction may be obtained which would not otherwise have been available. (Therefore, justice is served).
3. To lie to a suspect may be justified, provided that one does not go on to lie to the Crown Prosecution Service, Magistrate and Judge as to how the confession was obtained. If the case for the prosecution rests wholly or partly upon the use of deceptive tactics, then these must be declared and be open to evaluation. Provided that this tactic is declared, its use is not necessarily immoral.
4. In general terms, in this case the end could be argued to justify the means.

Against

1. Such an action may be in breach of procedures, whether internal or imposed by legislation such as PACE.
2. A conviction resting solely upon trickery and deception is unlikely to be safe. Indeed, under some legal systems, a confession alone is not enough to convict someone: there must be other evidence. This restriction does not apply under English law; nevertheless, it is a point to bear in mind.
3. If a confession obtained by trickery is simply a contributory factor to the case against someone, then the game may not be worth the

candle. Why risk bringing your whole case for the prosecution into potential disrepute, for the sake of this minor contribution?

4. Let us be explicitly ethical and say that this sort of behaviour is wrong, both absolutely and in terms of its consequences for the police themselves, and for their relationships with criminals, lawyers, and the public at large. Would you trust a liar? When is he lying, and when not?

5. We are creating a precedent which can lead to greater abuses. If we accept the possibility that lying to the prisoner can be justified, then we can put forward some very pretty scenarios, designed to put prisoners under pressure or in some other way deceive them: and in all cases, we could argue that if the interviewee were innocent, he would not make an admission. We could, for example:

☐ Disguise our police officer as a priest, and encourage the prisoner to make a confession of his sins, or cite others' guilt. (We may prepare for this by encouraging a prisoner or suspect to falsely believe that he is seriously ill or dying, and needs to make a confession.)

☐ Pretend to the prisoner or suspect that a loved one is ill or in danger, and that his cooperation will help them.

☐ Offer a reward of any kind for a confession or other information – the information being given, the reward is not forthcoming. After all, why should we complete a bargain with criminals, and hold to a code of honour with the dishonourable?

Comment

We stated earlier that an innocent person has nothing to fear. Experience indicates otherwise.

The Spanish fighting bull can only be used once in the arena, it is said, because if he were to repeat his part in the performance he would be wise to the tricks of the matador – which would presumably lead to a rather different result to the encounter, although not necessarily a less pleasing one to the crowd. However, it is not enough to argue that deception would soon prove self-defeating, since its potential victims would sooner or later be able to see through it, as the bull might see through the stratagems of his opponent.

We still need to resolve the issue of deception on ethical grounds. All of the examples are hypothetical, although instances of similar behaviour could be found in police history somewhere. I suppose that all of them would be condemned as improper behaviour by a judge: and all of them are unethical. Why?

It is wrong to break an agreement, even with a criminal. It is our honour which is at stake: not theirs.

Some acts are wrong in themselves. It is wrong to pretend to be a priest, doctor, counsellor or anyone else who can relieve pain and suffering, under circumstances where the person who is being deceived will adopt a dependent relationship to the deceiver, and in which the deceiver can exploit the other's credulity in ways of which they, and others, would disapprove if the truth were known. The short expression for this is manipulation.

Generally speaking, it is wrong to pretend to be anything that one is not. However, if we were to make that a universal principle then not only would acting and fancy dress parties become illegal, but no police officer would be able to engage in any form of deception, whether active or passive, as discussed in our section on the use of informants. We do not wish to go that far. Harmless deception, as for example play-acting, adds to the merriment of nations and would only be condemned by the most puritanical kill-joy. Moreover, such deceptions are a half-way house between reality and true deception. As Coleridge put it, we do not believe that an actor is really Hamlet: we suspend our disbelief that he is not. Actor and audience engage in a game, with rules which operate to their mutual benefit.

In the examples cited above, the benefit is rather one-sided.

Conclusion

We have explored this sort of deception in some depth, as it is an area in which police actions have sometimes brought the force into disrepute: and that is probably the strongest argument against it. It is the role of the police, as we established earlier, to investigate crime, and not to find ways of deceiving its real or supposed perpetrators. Let us ask the police officer who contemplates this type of deception some simple questions.

Do you wish to be a member of an organization which operates in this way?

Is that why you joined? Is that how you wish the public to see the police?

. . . .

Deception and entrapment

There is a grey area where a police officer pretends to be a criminal, or to be criminally inclined, in order to pursue his real occupation more effectively. Is this immoral? Not necessarily. Consider these two cases.

A. Police officers in plain clothes offer televisions and other attractive items for sale at nominal prices, in a public house chosen at random in a poorer part of town. Some members of the public show an interest. When they wonder at the prices, they are told that the goods suffered from excessive gravitational forces while in transit. In other words, they fell off the back of a lorry. Money changes hands. Charges relating to handling stolen goods are preferred.

B. A businessman (it is always a businessman, doctor, lawyer, or some other professional: other people do their dirty work for themselves, but a professional instinctively recognizes the right to specialize) wants his wife dead, but cannot bring himself to murder her himself, or would prefer that the crime did not lead to his door. He wants to employ a professional assassin. The police hear of this, and a policeman pretending to be an assassin deceives the businessman into revealing his criminal intent, recording the conversation on a concealed tape-recorder. The businessman is charged with plotting to murder his wife.

☐ Which case do you think will stand up in court?
☐ Which case is ethically acceptable?

Discussion

B wins over A.

In general terms, crime requires means, motive and opportunity.

In A, the means and opportunity to commit a crime have been artificially created. The motivation was there, but the *mens rea* or guilty mind was weak, the would-be purchasers being weak, foolish or gullible rather than natural-born criminals. Moreover, it is not the role of the police to create crime simply in order that they may solve it – however tempting this may be for someone who wishes to demonstrate his powers of detection.

In B, the crime was already in action: the businessman was seeking the means. Moreover, if the policeman had not been so obliging the wife would be dead, since a genuine assassin would presumably have been found.

These two cases are relatively simple, and their legal and moral stitching can be comparatively easily unpicked. Some forms of deception in this area are much more complex; and there is neither an overall legal ruling nor a simple moral catechism which can be applied. The astute police officer will do well to review past cases creating legal precedents, and build up his wisdom empirically. The cases will provide useful examples of both legal and moral reasoning which he may then use as a basis for deciding whether he should put into effect whatever is his own ploy. In addition, some reading is recommended. Our conclusions are as follows:

☐ There are instances where the end justifies the means.
☐ Under certain circumstances, police officers may set out to deceive.
☐ If deception is to be employed, it must be done professionally.
☐ Since deception involves lying, some police officers need to be accomplished liars, but not in the interview or court-room.

CORRUPTION

We started this chapter by considering the possibility that the police could prevent crime altogether. We recognized that not all crime can be prevented; that the police need to actively investigate crime, before, during and after its committal; and that this sows the prairie with inescapable moral dilemmas. As a finale to this chapter we shall consider police corruption, which I shall define as the systematic abuse or misuse of one's official power, status or position. (The Independent Commission Against Corruption of Hong Kong [ICAC], a body I greatly respected, defined corrupt behaviour as 'to act or refrain from acting in one's official capacity as a result of being offered or having solicited or accepted an advantage'. However, I prefer a wider definition.)

If we believe that everyone has his price, then any police officer could be corrupted, but members of CID or other specialist units are particularly vulnerable to corruption, for very obvious reasons. First, they have the means, motive and opportunity to practise so-called noble cause corruption, since it is they who investigate the activities of recalcitrant criminals and prepare the case against them. Secondly, it is CID which is most vulnerable to 'normal' corruption – ie the abuse or misuse of police power for personal gain – since CID, once again, has the greatest opportunities. It is no coincidence that corruption tends to be found where crimes such as drugs or pornography are concerned. The officer may see little result for his efforts. He may have reached a stage of moral outrage fatigue, and have simply lost interest in what he is supposed to be doing: especially if no victim is apparent, or there are problems with legal definition, as with obscene publications. And, of course, the criminal will have a strong interest in corrupting the investigator, and a finite number of investigators to corrupt, together with considerable assets to achieve his objective. Under such circumstances, we cannot expect zero corruption. The important thing is not that a force claims to be incorruptible, but what it does to investigate and foreclose the corruption it discovers through systematic and regular internal scrutiny.

Dealing with corruption

We may deal with corruption as a whole, since it is the misuse or abuse of one's official powers which is its defining characteristic, and not the reason for that misuse. Having first of all established that we must continually expect corruption even where there is no overt sign of its presence, we must consider what to do about it. Investigating corruption, once it is known or believed to be occurring, requires the same skills as investigating any other crime – with the proviso that those whose profession is to investigate their colleagues cannot always expect to be loved by them. Let us look at prevention, or rather, to be more realistic, the minimization of corruption.

Security

Valuable items need to be protected against internal as well as external theft or abuse. The security of information can be a problem, in that as Goffman (1970) so deftly explores, it can be breached without being removed. Computer security systems exist to prevent unauthorized access, and while the astute abuser can usually steal a tactical advantage, the system's designer should retain strategic superiority. A security expert will tell you that a system will probably be breached more often through operator carelessness or laziness, than through an inherent fault in its design; and standard (but not predictable) security measures will prevent many abuses if properly applied.

Active supervision

Any competent bank manager can explain how to set up a system to reduce fraud, embezzlement, and simple mistakes. No one should work without any form of supervision, and no one should be able to handle money, information, or any other scarce and potentially valuable property such as seized stolen goods or drugs, alone and without scrutiny by others.

Change

Predictability and routine make corruption easier. For a graphic illustration of this, see any second world war escape film, in which the (predictable) movements of sentries are studied and exploited.

Redefinition

To make drugs, obscene publications, or other sought-after but prohibited items legal, is immediately to remove a major potential cause of corruption. The police do not decide what should or should not be legal, but they can lobby those who do. As elsewhere, motive is important here: there is a difference between lobbying to decriminalize something because it would make your work easier, and lobbying to achieve the same end because you believe it to be right.

Pay and status

In some countries it might almost be said that police officers are corrupt because they have to be, since their official wages are so low, or irregularly paid, or both. It is a sensible policy to reduce the possibility of corruption by paying a wage that a police officer can live on, so that he does not have to look elsewhere for money or favours. Corruption can begin in very minor ways, and for police officers there is no such thing as a free meal.

Raising the moral level

The measures we have been describing so far are pragmatic. They make the abuse or misuse of power more difficult, by imposing constraints upon it, or by raising the threshold of temptation for the average potential abuser. (We might add exemplary punishments for those caught offending.) Another way to attack the problem is by the overt use of morality. We may select police officers who are less likely to be corrupted; train them more vigorously in the perils and temptations of corruption, and develop their moral fibre to resist it; or attempt to raise the moral standing and status of the occupation of policing as a whole, by such means as the publication of a moral code. In the opinion of experienced ICAC investigators, such options should certainly be tried, and are best linked to pragmatic measures which make corruption more difficult to practise and easier to detect. We go on to discuss ethical codes and their uses in later chapters.

ANNEXES

Home Office guidelines on the use of informants

No public informant should counsel, incite, or procure the commission of a crime. When an informant gives the police information about the intention of others to commit a crime in which they intend he shall play a part, his participation should be allowed to continue only where:
i.   he does not actively engage in planing and committing the crime
ii.   he is intended to play only a minor role
iii. his participation is essential to enable the police to frustrate the principal criminals and to arrest them....
The police must never commit themselves to a course which, whether to protect an informant or otherwise, will constrain them to mislead a court in any subsequent proceedings.'

(Levi, 1995)

Blackmail

Section 21, Theft Act, 1968:

A person is guilty of blackmail if, with a view to gain for himself or another, or with intent to cause loss to another he makes any unwarranted demand with menaces. And for this purpose a demand with menaces is unwarranted unless the person making it does so in the belief that a) he has reasonable grounds for making the demand and b) the use of the menaces is a proper means of reinforcing that demand.

Suppose a thief (A) steals a briefcase from a businessman (B)'s house, and finds it contains photographs of B taking part in sexual activities with children. A then writes to B, saying that unless he is paid £50,000, he will show the photographs to B's wife.

Is A guilty of blackmail? Yes.

- ☐ His letter was sent with a view to gain.
- ☐ It contains a demand.
- ☐ The demand is unwarranted.
- ☐ A menace exists.

Suppose a motorist (who is known to associate with some very bad people, but leads an apparently respectable life) is stopped for drunken driving. He is extremely anxious not to lose his licence, since his livelihood depends on it. A police officer says to him that he will be prosecuted unless he cooperates. How is he to cooperate? By becoming a police informant.

Is the police officer guilty of blackmail?

- ☐ The police officer does not stand to gain, since gain in this context has been construed as referring to money or other property. (If the police officer gains an informant, he will have a greater insight into the activities of a criminal gang. If he is paid performance-related pay, then it could be argued that he stands to gain in financial terms, from cultivating an informant. However, that is not usually the case.)
- ☐ He is making a demand.
- ☐ The demand is unwarranted.
- ☐ A menace exists.

Clearly the police officer is not guilty of blackmail, because of the lack of financial gain.

Is his behaviour justified? Could he be charged with other offences? I leave you to take your inquiries further!

4
A SHORT HISTORY OF POLICE ETHICS

THE POLICE SERVICE: A PROFESSION?

1. The British police service is, or aspires to be, a profession.
2. One of the defining characteristics of a profession is its declaration of an ethical code.
3. Therefore, the British police service must either be in the process of declaring an ethical code, or have already declared one

This interesting syllogism deserves exploration. I propose to deal with the middle proposition first. What is a profession?

A profession may be defined ironically (prostitution is quoted as the oldest profession) but in that case I think we are simply referring to what someone does for a living, and for which they expect to be paid. Those are not sufficient qualifications for a profession. A profession may be defined in three ways: historically, by analysis, or simply by accepting the statement of a group of people that this word applies to them. The third method may sound the least satisfactory, but I suspect that we shall come back to it in the end!

Medicine, the law and the church are cited by the *Shorter Oxford English Dictionary* as the traditional learned professions, with the army also mentioned as a profession – but presumably not a learned one. Let us leave aside the army for the time being, and look at the other three. If we take an historical, predominantly nineteenth century perspective, what did medicine, the law and the church have in common? I would suggest the following:

☐ They were all practised by gentlemen, or at least by people who aspired to that class.
☐ They were occupations of both status and prestige.

☐ They required preparatory study at university, so as to obtain the requisite qualifications.

☐ They resented competition, and did their best to create and maintain a monopoly.

If we assess policing against the traditional model of a profession, it fails. Modern policing stems from the Victorian period. The Metropolitan Police was founded by Sir Robert Peel in 1829, and by 1860 there were 226 other forces. How were they to be commanded? One of the things that Peel made clear from the start was that he did not see policing as an occupation for gentlemen; and he turned down applications from such as applied to command the new force. The New Police Establishment of 1829 had no officer class. The two commissioners were undoubtedly gentlemen, and both of them came from traditional professions. Charles Warren was a solicitor and Richard Mayne a soldier. The first receiver, in charge of property and fixtures, was also a solicitor with financial experience. Where it came to appointing the superintendents, Peel, Warren and Mayne favoured such candidates as ex-military warrant officers, presumably because they were considered to be experienced in handling and organizing men, and knew their place in society. They could be expected to command quietly and expeditiously, and not to think for themselves – for example, by challenging the moral outlook of their superiors. Peel did not set out to create a new profession, but a mechanism for social control which would be accepted by all classes. The constables' work was intended as mainly preventative – they patrolled London on fixed beats, under quasi-military supervision – and their role was clearly to keep the dangerous classes under control. New units were added reluctantly, and only when needed: CID in 1846, and Special Branch, as the Special Irish Branch, in 1886. Although CID was seen as an elite, detectives and their commanders were recruited from the same background as uniformed constables.

County police forces followed the same pattern. The chief constable might be from the landed gentry (some were appointed from the army in their twenties, and managed to remain in office for 50 or 60 years) but the officers under his command were not. The model of command in these cases was benevolent paternalism.

The new experiment succeeded, and the new Peelers became accepted, on the whole, for what they were intended to be: a civil police force. Tactics counted: and police acceptability grew as they were able to demonstrate that it was possible to police gatherings and demonstrations with patience, good humour and discipline, and without the use of excessive force.

Acceptability, however, is not the same as prestige. The police service is the child of its ancestors, and has made only limited attempts to raise its social status. Although the police service now recruits graduates, practises an accelerated promotion scheme, and devotes a good deal of time and money to attempting to ensure that its leaders have been thoroughly trained (it is possible for senior police officers to have spent a significant part of their service on courses, visits and attachments, rather than on operational policing) there has been little or no attempt at gentrification, and the service remains resolutely egalitarian, with no officer class.

The Trenchard Scheme

The Trenchard Scheme has been the only sustained attempt to create a leadership elite. This scheme was introduced into the Metropolitan Police in 1934 by Lord Trenchard, Commissioner of the Metropolitan Police from 1931 to 1935, and a former Marshal of the Royal Air Force. He described himself as 'an old man in a hurry'. Lord Trenchard believed that the police needed an officer class, and set out to create one, beginning with the Metropolitan Police. In 1934, 35 young men began a special course at the Metropolitan Police Training Centre in Hendon, designed to equip them to be the police leaders of the future. It is noteworthy that although Lord Trenchard set out to create an officer class he did not confine his search for prospective leaders to the schools and universities, and that 21 of the total of 35 candidates chosen were already in the police service. The course lasted 15 months, of which six were spent on the beat. Trenchard left the police in 1935, and his plan withered with the beginning of the second world war. The police service has never re-attempted the creation of an officer class.

If we set out to analyse the Trenchard Scheme, what do we discover?

☐ The scheme was short lived. It lasted from 1934 to 1940 and has never been revived. The present accelerated promotion scheme run by the police bears little relation to it.
☐ Numbers were limited. The majority of police leaders were never products of the Trenchard Scheme.

☐ Some impact was made. According to Lord Trenchard's biographer, of the 197 officers graduating from the Trenchard scheme, nearly a third rose to the highest ranks in Great Britain and the Commonwealth. He wrote in 1962 that their number included the then Metropolitan Police Commissioner, Sir Joseph Simpson, and 20 provincial chief constables. Was the police service seen to be more professional, under their command? A fascinating question, and impossible to answer!

☐ The Trenchard Scheme did not create an officer class. Cadets included young men who were already serving police officers, as well as outsiders. In other words, the Trenchard Scheme served to identify, develop and promote talent within the police service, as well as or more than to inject it from outside.

☐ The Trenchard Scheme was profoundly unpopular in police culture and mythology, which is strongly egalitarian. Most police officers value experience, and want their service to be commanded by people who join as ordinary constables.

Overseas, of course, it was all rather different. Our colonies, dominions and other overseas possessions were policed by para-military forces – if not by the army itself – and these forces did have an officer class. It was, of course, white. It is doubtful if it could claim professional status. Colonial policing does not appear to have been an occupation for gentlemen.

Review

We have explored the traditional notion of a learned profession at some length, and decided that not only did the police not measure up to it, but that:

☐ the police service was deliberately moulded in another image; and
☐ very probably, its practitioners would not have wished for professional status in any case. Police officers were not recruited from the upper and middle classes, did not study at university, and did not aspire to social prestige.

So far our analysis has been strongly historical. The church, the law, the medical profession and the army are quite different from what they were in the nineteenth century; and there are now many other groups claiming professional status. Perhaps we should be attempting to define what makes a profession, in terms other than the social position of its members.

The characteristics of a modern profession

According to the sociologist Norman Greenhill (1985) a profession has four characteristics:

- [ ] The work is of social value.
- [ ] The occupation develops a unique body of knowledge.
- [ ] The occupation restricts entry.
- [ ] The occupation disciplines itself.

How does the police service compare with this?

Social value

Police work is clearly of social value. However, this may not be as useful a criterion as it at first appears. Whatever their occupation, from parson to pornographer, most people could argue that their work is of social value. It is a loose phrase which lends itself to unfalsifiable claims. Away with it!

A unique body of knowledge

I enter this area with great trepidation. It is easy to exaggerate the professional knowledge required of the police officer, and equally easy to underestimate or even dismiss the skills it requires to be one. The first problem is to agree what we mean by knowledge. Let me put forward two propositions.

1. A unique body of knowledge can only be recognized if it is intellectually based and recorded.
2. We can only be sure that knowledge has been transmitted to new professionals if they have undergone formal teaching and sat an examination.

Would-be doctors, lawyers and accountants (to expand our traditional framework a little) need to master a good deal of formal learning to enter their profession, and may take further knowledge-based professional examinations as they progress through it.

Police officers follow a very different path. The knowledge which they have to acquire is not, on the whole, unique to their profession;

and they do not have to engage in formal study to gain it. Indeed, much practical policing wisdom could not be studied at all, in an academic sense, for it is not written down. Interestingly, when police forces do try to professionalize themselves, and decide that police recruits must study for lengthy periods before they can go on the beat, the subjects they are to study are chosen from other disciplines. Would-be police officers study first aid, law and sociology. They learn about communications, traffic and firearms. They may even practise 'interpersonal skills'. But they do not study policing, because they cannot. It is not transcribed.

There is an art to police work, and it is easy to get it wrong. A police officer can cause or prevent a riot, simply by the way he handles a crowd, or even an individual. Good police officers need an insight into human behaviour under stress: but that insight does not constitute a unique body of knowledge. Police officers share in other peoples' knowledge. They need an understanding of human behaviour, but not a degree in psychology. They need a reasonable knowledge of the law, but not to be legally qualified. They would be well advised to have a good grasp of first aid, since they are often first to arrive at the incident which requires it, but they do not need a medical qualification. The police officer needs sufficient knowledge to be able to do his job. He does not have to put the seal of uniqueness upon that knowledge. As he goes further in his trade he needs to be able to understand other peoples's skills, hobbies and interests, in order to know what motivates and demotivates them, but his understanding is human rather than technical. A civil engineer, let us say, designs a bridge. He needs to know all about stresses, strains and bearing loads in order to be able to do his job. A police officer investigates the engineer, to find out if he murdered his wife. He, also, needs to know about stresses and strains, but not on the bridge. His job is to understand the engineer.

Police examinations
Traditionally, police constables have been promoted to sergeant and inspector by virtue of passing an examination designed to test their knowledge of the law and police duties. Police examinations are practically based. They are designed to explore an operator's grasp of those parts of a complex subject which he needs to be able to understand in order to do his job – which includes supervision. The sergeant or inspector is expected not only to have a reasonable working grasp of the law for himself, but to be able to advise, help and

guide his constables in its application. Suppose a police examination is exploring the topic of powers of arrest. It seeks to find out the candidate's knowledge of the law, and whether or not he can apply that knowledge in unfamiliar or complex circumstances. It does not ask for his views on police powers of arrest in term of their origins, reasonableness and alternatives. He is not required to display original thought. There is no suggestion of an essay. In other words, it is not an academic exercise. Police examinations are not intended to test whether or not candidates have mastered a body of knowledge unique to policing, and they do not form part of the process of socialization which is so important to a true profession.

Skills-based testing
It is noteworthy that the new trend in police examinations is moving further and further away from the traditional academic pattern. In addition to a traditional test of his knowledge of the law, the contemporary would-be sergeant undergoes a series of tests named OSPRE, designed by other police officers working at a central planning and training unit in Harrogate. The OSPRE candidate is expected to demonstrate practical policing and supervisory skills, which are assessed by observation. In other words, this is something like a driving test, only with people rather than vehicles.

Where detection meets science
The good police officer, and particularly the good detective, needs a working knowledge of some aspects of other professions if he is to pursue his own successfully. Where detection meets science, the detective may acquire a highly specialized knowledge. When DNA profiling was developed by Alex Jeffreys at Leicester University, local detectives were among the first to take an interest – because they could see the possible practical implications of the discovery, in terms of identifying murderers, rapists and other criminals. A second example of a specialized interest is investigative psychology. The scientist uses a range of techniques to analyse a range of apparently disconnected crimes. He then infers whether or not a 'serial' killer or rapist is involved in those crimes, and goes on to draw up an offender profile: a portrait of the offender in terms of identifiable characteristics. While various psychologists have assisted the police in their enquiries, as the phrase has it, offender profiling is probably most strongly associated with the work of Professor David Canter, of Liverpool University.

There are a number of police officers, some with little or no previous academic background or experience, who have become extremely adept in the science of offender profiling, and have mastered a good deal of scientific methodology in order to achieve this, to do with statistics, computational analysis, and so on. However, they have remained police officers first and scientists second, and their interest in investigative psychology has been a practical one.

Restricted entry

The police service is successful in restricting entry. Police forces set and enforce standards as to who may join the occupation and who may not. Those standards are fair, in the broadest sense: in other words, openly known, appropriate for the task in hand, and reasonably easy to apply. Equal opportunities legislation has made recruiting officers think much harder about their criteria for recruitment, since they may now be challenged at tribunal. Do you need to be six foot tall in order to be a successful constable? Clearly, the answer is no, and height restrictions have been largely removed. Necessary criteria have been retained. They do not include academic qualifications. Police officers have traditionally been chosen for their robust physique, necessary motivation and good character, rather than brains, and the tradition continues. It is an axiom of police recruiting that the service should represent the society that it polices, and graduates are represented but not over-represented in the police service.

Self-discipline

Police officers, like other citizens, are accountable to the law. In addition, the police service disciplines itself. Police officers are subject to a discipline code which contains offences not in the criminal code; bringing the force into disrepute, for example. Complaints against the police used to be investigated purely by police officers. Nowadays there is an independent body to oversee this, the Police Complaints Authority, whose title is self-explanatory; but I do not think its existence can be said to weaken the professional status of the police service very seriously. The police service is now considering how to revise its discipline code, and I shall return to this point. What is clear, however, is that the service will not give up the right to discipline itself.

....

Review: what is a profession?

We have looked at the defining characteristics of a profession, and decided that the police measure up quite well on some factors, but have a problem over knowledge. Before we become inextricably entangled in this thicket, let us remember what we are really supposed to be researching: the police attitude to ethics and in particular their acceptance or rejection of an ethical code.

Our first proposition was this: that the declaration of an ethical code is one of the defining characteristics of a profession. This is simply untrue. The more that one tries to define a profession, the more difficult it becomes. In the end, analysis becomes self-defeating, and we go back to history. Occupations traditionally known as professions have not always declared an ethical code, and the Hippocratic Oath is the exception and not the rule. I would rest my case, except that circumstances are changing. More and more occupations are attempting to professionalize themselves, and declaring an ethical code is seen as a desirable if not essential part of this process.

The police attitude to professionalization is deeply ambivalent. There are police officers who want their occupation to become a profession, with all that this entails. We may assume that this group includes some but not all senior police officers. There are others who have no wish to be categorized with the traditional professions or their contemporary emulators. The professionalizers, as it were, are committed to an ethical code – or perhaps to a combination of ethics and discipline. The position of the opposition is less easily delineated.

PROFESSIONS AND PROFESSIONALISM

The word 'profession' may be contrasted with trade, craft, or occupation.

The word 'professional' contrasts with 'amateur'. Every regular police officer wants to see himself as professional rather than an amateur in his work, because amateur is taken to mean slipshod, careless, and clumsy – the enthusiastic amateur who gets in the way.

Leave it to us. We're the professionals

There is a sub-text to this. Professionals are paid for their labour, and amateurs are not. The government wants to make much more use of the special constabulary – the amateur part of the professional police force. Specials wear a uniform and work alongside regular police officers, but are unpaid. The regular's attitude to his or her part time colleague is ambivalent. The individual special, as a person, may be seen as anything from a useful asset to a general liability, better left at the station and answering the telephone. (A dubious policy, since getting the initial information right is sometimes rather useful.) In general, the special is likely to be seen as a threat: policing on the cheap. While it is easy for the professional to decry the efforts of the amateur, the underlying emotion may be fear rather than arrogance. Some people – actors, sportsmen, local politicians and lay readers are obvious examples – may do something for the love of it, without expecting payment. These amateurs are not necessarily amateurish. Amateur actors or footballers may out-perform professionals. Special constables would be a potential threat to professional police officers – if their enthusiasm and skills could be used to reduce the number of paid officers.

THE BRITISH POLICE SERVICE: MOVES TOWARDS PROFESSIONALISM

The British police service has made a number of efforts to be explicit about the values it holds and the ethical principles by which it operates. Let us examine four examples, in terms of one tradition and three reforms.

The constable's oath

Every new police officer swears the following oath, traditional to the service:

> I solemnly and sincerely declare and affirm that I will well and truly serve our Sovereign Lady the Queen in the Office of Constable without favour or affection, fear or ill-will, and that I will, to the best of my power, cause the peace to be kept and preserved, and prevent all offences against the person and properties of Her Majesty's subjects, and that while I continue to hold the said office I will, to the best of my skill and knowledge, discharge all the duties thereof faithfully according to law.

This oath pre-dates any attempt to make the police a professional organization, like the medical profession. In one sense, it means that they are already professionals. Is the oath sufficient to be an ethical code, or must it be augmented? That is debatable.

The Principles of Policing and Guidance for Professional Behaviour

On 1 April 1985 the Metropolitan Police produced a short handbook entitled as above. Its last two pages contained a 'Code of professional duties', consisting of five 'duties of function' and four 'duties of method'. Whether or not the then Commissioner, Sir Kenneth Newman, intended this code to become a national point of reference, I do not know. In any case, it did not succeed. Whatever its merits, the handbook had little impact.

The Police Service Statement of Common Purpose and Values

The Metropolitan Police – the largest force in the United Kingdom, and the one most subject to criticism – next attempted a programme of internal reform which was called the PLUS programme. This did have consequences: its Statement of Common Purpose and Values was adopted as a national document.

> The purpose of the police service is to uphold the law fairly and firmly; to prevent crime; to pursue and bring to justice those who break the law; to keep the Queen's Peace; to protect, help, and reassure the community; and to be seen to do all this with integrity, common sense, and sound judgment.
>
> We must be compassionate, courteous and patient, acting without fear or favour or prejudice to the rights of others. We need to be professional, calm and restrained in the face of violence and apply only that force which is necessary to accomplish our lawful duty.
>
> We must strive to reduce the fears of the public and, so far as we can, reflect their priorities in the action we take. We must respond to well-founded criticism with a willingness to change.

This statement indicates that the police define their objectives very broadly, and relate what they are able to achieve to how they are perceived. It is the statement of an organization which believes in policing by consent, knows that it cannot solve crimes without the public's cooperation, and emphasizes its civilian rather than para-military characteristics. Is it the statement of an aspiring profession? That proposition remains unproven. To issue such a statement is neither necessary nor sufficient to achieve professional status. Other things being equal, it may help.

A police ethical code?

A police service statement of ethical principles was issued in 1992. It said:

As a member of the Police Service, I will:-

1. Act with fairness, carrying out my responsibilities with integrity and impartiality.
2. Perform my duties with diligence and a proper use of discretion.
3. In my dealings with all individuals, both outside and inside the Police Service, display self control, tolerance, understanding, and courtesy appropriate to the circumstances.
4. Uphold fundamental human rights, treating every person as an individual and display respect and compassion towards them.
5. Support all my colleagues in the performance of their lawful duties and in doing so, actively oppose and draw attention to any malpractice by any person.
6. Respect the fact that much of the information I receive is confidential and may only be divulged when my duty requires me to do so.
7. Exercise force only when justified and use only the minimum amount of force necessary to effect my lawful purpose and restore the peace.
8. Act only within the law, in the understanding that I have no authority to depart from due legal process and that no one may place a requirement on me to do so.
9. Use resources entrusted to me to the maximum benefit of the public.
10. Accept my responsibility for self development, continually seeking to improve the way in which I serve the community.
11. Accept personal accountability for my own acts and omissions.

For various reasons the statement did not meet with general acceptance from the police. Some, no doubt, felt that they could do a better draft. Some were opposed to the whole idea, for the reasons we have already mentioned. And some were worried that if the police drafted and agreed an ethical code, it would have legal implications. In other words, although the code was intended only to guide behaviour, failure to comply with it could be quoted by lawyers as evidence of misconduct.

We are begging a rather large question here, since if a police code of ethics is to be accepted by the public as a meaningful document, then it *should* be quotable by lawyers. However, the story is not over yet. There are two further twists.

Revision

Four years later, the police service statement of ethical principles has become a draft statement of police shared values, and the 11 principles are now eight. Police officers now promise to:

1. Treat everyone with respect by upholding fundamental human rights in accordance with law.
2 Act only within the law and resist pressure to do otherwise.
3. Act with fairness, impartiality and integrity.
4. Exercise self-control and understanding with appropriate tolerance and courtesy.
5. Use discretion properly.
6. Improve our service to the community through diligence and continuous personal development.
7. Support our colleagues in their lawful duties, but actively oppose any wrongdoing.
8. Acknowledge accountability for our acts and omissions.

Compared with the original, this is a sparse and uninspiring document, which gives off a strong whiff of having been put together (I hesitate to say crafted) by a committee. It would appear to have been phrased so as not to cause offence to its readers, and its limp platitudes do not inspire. For the remainder of this chapter, where I refer to the police ethical code I have the 1992 version in mind.

Ethical and disciplinary codes compared

The police discipline code (as at 1996) lays out what the police cannot do, and its offences can be used as a basis for discipline. It is quoted in full in the Annex to this chapter. The traditional police discipline code and the 1992 draft code of professional ethics differ in substance, style and purpose. Although in some instances the same issues are referred to, it is in a different way. Even where there appears a similarity, for example in regard to the notion of the unacceptability of improper disclosure of information, the two codes have a different intention. The discipline code lays down what a police officer must not do. The code of ethics gives him an idea of the standard of behaviour he should aim for. In shorthand, one code is prohibitive, and the other aspirational.

As Lord Devlin pointed out, we should not think much of a man who based his conduct solely on what he was required to avoid; and there is clearly a need for an aspirational as well as a prohibitive code. Could the two be combined? I think not, since the result would surely achieve neither aim.

The police federation is rightly opposed to the idea that the discipline code could be replaced by an ethical code which is used for disciplinary purposes, within the police service. The ten commandments were prohibitive, whereas the message of the New Testament is aspirational. We need both: but there is no doubt which is more important.

SUMMARY AND CONCLUSION

The contemporary meaning of the word 'profession' is difficult if not impossible to define authoritatively. Nevertheless, we can say that the police service is not a profession in the traditional sense of the word. It remains more like a craft. For a variety of reasons, some of them to do with preserving the existence of professional policing as an integral part of the public service in an era of privatization, there is a move to further professionalize the police service.

As part of that move, and for other reasons, the police service is considering the adoption of a professional code of ethics. A code has been produced and revised, but not yet accepted.

The water has been muddied by the ongoing debate over the purpose and content of the police discipline code, the standard of proof required in administering it, and the alchemical dream of combining discipline and ethics.

There is a need for an ethical code as an aspirational document, and in the next chapter we shall articulate how it could be used. In the absence of the adoption of an ethical code, the police statement of common purpose and values is a useful but not complete substitute.

APPENDIX

The Police Discipline Code

The Code prohibits the following offences, of which I give only the headings, and not the definitions and remarks following them. This code is due to be republished in 1997.

1. Discreditable conduct
2. Misconduct towards a member of a police force
3. Disobedience to orders
4. Neglect of duty
5. Falsehood or prevarication
6. Improper disclosure of information
7. Corrupt or improper practice
8. Abuse of authority
9. Racially discriminatory behaviour
10. Neglect of health
11. Improper dress or untidiness
12. Damage to police property
13. Drunkenness
14. Drinking on duty or soliciting drink
15. Entering licensed premises
16. Criminal conduct
17. Being an accessory to a disciplinary offence.

5
ADOPTING AND USING A CODE OF ETHICS

In October 1992 Her Majesty's Chief Inspector of Constabulary, Sir John Woodcock, CBE, QPM, CBIM, stated at a police conference:

> I want to put the full weight of the Inspectorate behind the Code of Ethics for the Police Service, currently being developed.... The Statement of Common Purpose makes clear the mission of the Police Service, whereas the Code of Ethics is designed to provide individual officers with guidance as to their own professional behaviour.... I believe the Code is an excellent initiative and I want to make clear something about why it is being brought into existence and its purpose.
>
> It may well be asked as to why, 150 years after the service was established, it has suddenly found itself needing a Code of Ethics. The answer is that 20th century Britain is a multicultural society.... For the last several decades, the police may have been complacent in assuming a shared set of values among those whom it recruits; the purpose of the new Code is to make manifest the values that the organization demands from those in its ranks.
>
> That said, it is vital that the issue of the Code is not seen as expressing widespread dissatisfaction with the behaviour of officers currently serving. Its main purposes are, first, to confirm shared values among individuals and, secondly, to provide a method of decision-making for individuals facing difficult moral choices.
>
> The Code will make clear ... that the task of the police is not only to seek the truth but to tell the truth; that a deliberate breach of investigative procedure may be as serious a crime as the crime under investigation; that the integrity of the way in which police investigate crime and, indeed, other offences is at least as important as the success of the investigation....

With such weight behind the (draft) ethical code, why was it not immediately accepted? There are reasons to do with police organization and politics which form part of the answer. I should like to explore some deeper factors to do with how police officers see and go about their work.

POLICE WORK AS A CRAFT

Police work has been traditionally organized as a craft, and the craftsman works alone. The root metaphor of British policing is the village bobby. In North America, it is the small town sheriff. What do they have in common? They work alone. They make decisions by themselves. They do not consult. They are not advised. They can and do, in extremis, represent the law purely by themselves. In 'High Noon', when no one will help the sheriff, Gary Cooper takes on the forces of evil single-handed. (And his girl waits for him, having said she won't!) If they have an ethical code, it is undeclared, personal, and probably unique. It is not susceptible to scholarly analysis. It may be even be subconscious.

POLICE DISCRETION

The police service is a disciplined organization. Police officers wear uniforms, salute, and have been known to march. Where it is appropriate that senior officers direct their activities, they accept lawful orders. Comparisons are sometimes made between the police and the armed services, as if they were similar organizations. However, the assumption of police uniformity is misleading. Police constables have a strong element of discretion as to how they achieve their primary responsibility, which is to keep the peace on the basis of a pact with society: and they have an element of discretion as to when and how they apply the law. Discretion, personal accountability for one's actions, and individual decision making go together, so that a police officer is not necessarily inclined to perceive the potential benefits of an ethical code. Put simply, he has not previously consulted other officers as to the professional decisions he makes, so why should he consult them, simply because of the existence of an ethical code? The police at all levels are used to a system of individual decision making, wherein the role of the senior officer is to investigate any mistakes afterwards, rather than offer advice beforehand.

SOLIDARITY

Police officers perceive themselves to be (and sometimes are) a beleaguered minority, constantly scrutinized and criticized by everyone else. Under such circumstances, a police officer has a duty to support his colleagues, and certainly not to criticize their actions in public. Does this mean that no discussion can take place at all, and that police decision making is purely a private affair? Logically, no: police officers can still consult with their colleagues in private as to what they should do (or more likely, what they should have done). But if you put police officers in a group with no outsiders present, their first instinct is not to debate professional dilemmas, but to bond with each other. After all, there are a lot of enemies out there, and they need all the support they can muster.

Solidarity is an admirable characteristic in a Polish trade union standing up to state communism. It is less desirable in an organization which wishes to encourage free internal debate and open decision making. It can lead to misplaced loyalty and other faults, which we shall explore later.

THE PURPOSE OF AN ETHICAL CODE

An ethical code is a publicly expressed set of principles, by considering which a practitioner of the profession in question may decide upon the right course of action. We assume, naturally, that he will only need such a code where he faces a dilemma as to what to do, and where no other source, such as the law, exists to guide his action, or where any other source is so general as not to provide guidance.

How might an ethical principle be useful? Let us take the issue of force. Article 7 of the 1992 draft police ethical code states that:

> As a member of the police service, I will exercise force only when justified and use only the minimum amount of force necessary to effect my lawful purpose and restore the peace.

This is similar to what is written in other, widely accepted police ethical codes, such as those published by the United Nations and the Council of Europe. The Council's 1979 declaration on police ethics states under item 12:

> In performing his duties, a police officer shall use all necessary

determination to achieve an aim which is legally required or allowed, but he may never use more force than is reasonable.

The use of force is clearly an area which was a source of controversy long before the ethical code was formulated, and in which police officers have always sought guidance. The code does not say: Thou shalt not kill. That is a religious commandment. It is absolute, and police officers who kill in the course of their duties must reconcile their public actions with their private beliefs. A police officer who kills someone in the course of his duties has broken this commandment, but is not necessarily in breach of either the criminal law or the ethical code. If an armed robber threatens a member of the public or a police officer with his weapon, and if there is no alternative but to shoot him in order to protect life, then the police officer is entitled, after giving a warning which has been disregarded, to shoot him: and if he shoots him the robber may die. Minimum force may include lethal force.

This scenario is well known, and the ethical principles upon which it is based have often been applied to real-life situations, so that there is a body of recorded experience which can be drawn upon. Firearms teams know what they are allowed to do and what is not acceptable: indeed, they may have specific rules as to when they may or may not open fire. Some criminals have also studied the rules. It has been reported that some unhinged individuals will threaten to open fire with a shotgun, and then just as the police are about to open fire will lay the weapon down. No police officer can open fire while the weapon is on the ground, since no one's life is immediately in danger. Then the deranged person picks up the weapon again, knowing what he is doing; and the dance with death continues.

Does it matter if the firearm is real or a replica, a starting pistol, a weapon loaded with blanks, or the like? Not really. That may sound an extremely callous statement: but the test is what it was reasonable to believe at the time, and not what subsequently proves to have been true. If you wait until a criminal fires his weapon in order to establish whether or not it is genuine, you may have waited too long.

Firearms should only be used by officers who have been especially selected and trained, and whose competence and psychological suitability for their special responsibility is constantly reassessed. In the case of the Royal Ulster Constabulary, every male member of the force is in this category. Weapons have been withdrawn from officers, despite the possible security risk, who were judged to be not in a fit state to handle them. The number of RUC officers who have fired their personal protection weapons over the past 26 years is, I would suggest, surprisingly low. Most people who come under a surprise attack do not have time to shoot back.

THE FOUNDATIONS FOR THE POLICE ETHICAL CODE

The police service statement of ethical principles was not created in a vacuum. It is conventional to argue that western morality rests upon Judaeo-Christianity. Be that as it may, it is now commonplace to base ethical codes upon the (secular) notion of rights. The commentary which accompanied the launch of the 1992 police ethical code referred to the following documents, as foundation stones:

- [ ] The United Nations Declaration of Human Rights.
- [ ] The Council of Europe Convention on Human Rights.
- [ ] The United Nations Code of Conduct for Law Enforcement Officials.
- [ ] The Council of Europe Declaration on the Police.

I mention these foundations now because they are relevant to the issue of the use of deadly force. The Council of Europe Convention on Human Rights recognizes that life may be taken when it results from the use of force which is no more than is absolutely necessary:

a.   in defence of a person from unlawful violence;
b.   to effect lawful arrest;
c.   to prevent the escape of a person lawfully detained;
d.   in action lawfully taken to quell riot or insurrection.

Could it be the case that the British police, by considering the implications of the European Convention on Human Rights, would have greater powers to shoot wrong-doers than if they had never heard of the Convention? That would be a paradox indeed! As with every good paradox, however, I believe that the contradiction is more apparent than real. Let us take condition c). First, British police officers are not accustomed to shoot fleeing felons (and do not usually have the means to do so). Secondly, I think that we may safely assert that where two moral codes could be quoted so as to offer alternative advice, the purer should prevail. Thus, if a European Convention offers the possibility of the justified shooting of an escaping prisoner, whereas British custom

and usage would be wholly opposed to this, there is no doubt as to
which is the purer policy.

General use of force

The use of firearms is not the only situation in which a police officer
will have to use force. While the use of intentionally lethal force is
inevitably dramatic and headline-catching, and its consequences may
very well be permanent, it is the use of force in everyday police life
which creates the wide range of practical dilemmas in which ethical
guidance may be of most assistance.

Use of the truncheon or baton

A police officer hits a demonstrator with his truncheon during a riot.
The demonstrator has an especially weak skull, and dies from a blow
which a normal person would have withstood. Was that unnecessary
force? Not necessarily: and the investigator will want to know very
much more than I have contributed here.

Is the character of the police officer an issue? It must be. There are
officers who are constantly the subject of complaint, while others
appear to lead charmed lives. It is not necessarily the case that the
force-addicted officer has been less lucky, and dealt with more than his
share of violence, than his less-accused colleague. Some officers are
simply more clumsy and more inclined to use force than their peers,
and the astute investigator will regard the history, modus operandi, and
psychological state of the accused as relevant factors in evaluating
whether or not excessive force was used on a particular occasion.

The use of force by a criminal does not justify its use by the police. It
is not the case that if one person breaks a generally accepted moral
code, he has forsworn his own right to its protection. Moral codes are
universal, and Article 4 of the police ethical code refers specifically to
upholding fundamental human rights.

An extreme case

The United Nations Declaration of Human Rights refers to the right
not to be subjected to torture, or to cruel, inhuman or degrading
treatment. Therefore, one would suppose, the police have no right to

use force other than as defined under Article 7, and that is an end of the matter. But ethical analysis is not that simple.

Suppose A is a police office, B is a victim, C is a criminal – in this case, a kidnapper. It is easily possible to imagine circumstances under which the police officer, A, might be very sorely tempted to inflict pain on B in order to save C, even though B may not have caused A any pain, or be threatening anyone in his immediate vicinity. Suppose B has been kidnapped by C. Detective A arrests C, who admits he has kidnapped B, but refuses to say where she is hidden. He then gloats in informing A that B is hidden in a coffin buried in shallow earth, that she has a limited air supply, that she will die in a very short time, and that there is nothing he proposes to do to save her. His lips are now sealed. Hers soon will be.

Some of you will have already recognized this plot. Detective A is Dirty Harry, Inspector Harry Callaghan of the Los Angeles Police Department, who is portrayed by Clint Eastwood as an exemplary police officer: courageous, resolute, and confident in his own judgement – if a little addicted to the use of a .44 magnum revolver rather than detection to clear up crime in greater Los Angeles. Harry has discovered the kidnapper in an empty baseball stadium, at night. He has shot him in the leg while the kidnapper was attempting to escape, and is now standing over him while the kidnapper pleads for help. Harry's overweight partner appears – he was the one who thought that they needed a search warrant – and Inspector Callaghan utters the immortal words: 'Get some air, Fatso.'

He then grinds the kidnapper's wound with his foot. But it is all too late: the girl is dead. Moreover, the case against the kidnapper is destroyed by Harry's tactics, and he goes free – until the final act.

'Is what Harry does worthy of debate?'
'Yes. There is a dilemma here, and not just an example of wrong conduct.'
'Would I consider doing it?'
'Certainly. But it cannot be justified by any universally intended moral code.'
'Why not?'

1. It is proscribed under Articles 4 and 8 of the police ethical code, if not others. (It is also a disciplinary offence.) Whatever the reasoning, there can be no justification for inflicting pain. It is absolutely forbidden. And if that were not enough –

. . . .

2. There is a difficulty about knowledge. Can we be absolutely sure that this is the guilty person? Is the girl's life really in danger? Is there genuinely so little time that almost anything is justified? Is there no alternative way of finding out what we need to know?

3. Is torture, whether by commission or omission, likely to lead to the result that we want? It is often asserted that people being tortured will simply say what the torturer appears to want to hear, and that this method is unlikely to lead to the truth.

4. Imagine the consequences if police officers were advised that they could, under carefully defined circumstances, inflict pain to discover the truth. Better to proscribe this activity altogether, and deal with cases where the code was broken on their merits, than to encourage the attitude that inflicting pain is another option in the toolkit. Torture is a tool of last resort, to be used, if at all, in the knowledge that its use is both wrong in itself and detrimental to the user.

In his study *The Rebel*, Albert Camus argues that certain acts (he discusses tyrannicide in nineteenth century Russia) are both necessary and inexcusable. Camus describes Russian assassins welcoming death on the scaffold as a liberation for what they have done.

Some variations

A. Torture may be mental as well as physical, and ingenuity is not a substitute for sound moral judgement. Here is a shorter vignette.

> *Police officer: 'Your wife is desperately ill. Give us the information we need, and we will save her.'*
> Criminal: 'I'll do it.'

She is not ill. Is this mental torture? Modern judges might say yes, although I suspect that their predecessors would have been more robust about this. Some philosophers or religious leaders, Kant, for example, would argue the extreme view that deception is wrong in itself, for any reason. The ethics of lying have been examined in depth by Sissela Bok (1978). She argues that contrary to popular thinking, lying is rarely justified; what needs to be established is a climate in which telling the truth is acceptable. The author gives examples in Chapters 8, 9 and 10 (lies in crisis; lying to liars; lying to enemies) of occasions when it may be permissible to lie. Mrs Bok presents a strong analysis across a range of instances and her book is worth reading.

Rather than dictating absolutes she asks pragmatic questions:

What consequences could follow from your lie? How likely are they? What climate is it likely to establish for your organization?

B. A police officer might argue that he is entitled to consider inflicting pain, whether physical or mental, or at least to prevent its relief, if the well-being of a large number of people be contrasted with the suffering of one person. In effect, he would be suggesting a utilitarian calculation. Suppose you have arrested an animal rights activist, who claims to have poisoned a large amount of food in a popular supermarket. He is not prepared to tell you any more, and if what he says is true a large number of people may die. Are you entitled to inflict pain, to discover the truth? In this extreme example, although the same questions about knowledge could be asked as in the Dirty Harry scenario, I suspect that a number of people would agree that pain was justified.

C. Suppose one further twist. The poisoner says to you: 'Yes, I know where the poison is, and I will tell you. But first you must release my friend from custody.'

In effect, this is blackmail by threat of terror. Is the police officer morally obliged to keep his word, if he agrees to release the poisoner's friend so as to save the innocent people who might otherwise have been poisoned? Legally, he is not obliged to do so; a contract made under duress is not a contract. Morally, it could be argued either way. Some would say that a promise is a promise, and that one should keep one's word under any circumstances. I would not agree. This is a case where deception is justified: 'Yes, I will release your friend. Trust me.'

In my reading, this sort of deception does not require a revision of the moral code, which makes no reference to the need for absolute truth and fidelity.

A moral code covering every possible combination of circumstances would be impossibly prolix and defeat its purpose. It must remain general and capable of interpretation. It is there for guidance. Discussing extreme hypothetical cases as well as everyday moral dilemmas will enable a group of police officers to recognize and clarify the basis upon which they make practical decisions.

IRISH TERRORISM AND THE ROLE OF THE POLICE

The present troubles in Northern Ireland began in 1969, a previous and very much smaller campaign of largely rural violence having petered out at the beginning of the 1960s. The Royal Ulster Constabulary was an old-fashioned force in 1969, and its officers faced great difficulties. The skills they possessed – the RUC was a paramilitary force, and they had had extensive weapons training – were unsuited for dealing with a civil rights campaign which was spilling over into street disorder and casual violence. What they lacked – proper intelligence gathering, coping with public disorder without resort to firearms, and an active public relations strategy – would have been extremely useful to them.

Since 1969 we have seen the development of a vicious campaign of murder, bombings and shootings, in which huge numbers of innocent people have been killed, maimed or otherwise damaged, including the largely Catholic victims of the UVF. The army was rapidly called in, but war or a state of siege was never declared. Internment and detention (the same thing under another name) were tried and abandoned. Stormont, the Northern Irish parliament, was prorogued, and the immensely powerful Special Powers Act was abolished: no longer could the Minister of Home Affairs act as he chose. Indeed, his office no longer existed. Westminster imposed and retains direct rule.

Under these conditions, some people would argue (they did, and do – and it can be phrased as a moral argument) that anything goes. The IRA and UVF put themselves beyond the pale. They deserve whatever they get. You do not cope with war as you cope with peace, and the strategy and tactics of policing by consent in a liberal democracy are inappropriate for dealing with a sustained campaign of terror whose object is to overthrow the state. The first duty of a state is to protect the lives of its citizens, and the British government has failed to do this, through eschewing robust tactics of counter-terrorism.

The essence of the argument is this: peace and war are different, and require different moral codes. It is overstated to say that in war anything is permissible – there were criteria for a just war developed in medieval times, and there are war crimes now – but it is clearly true that in war the doctrine of minimum force is a nonsense. War is about the application of maximum force at the enemy's weakest point, a principle the IRA understands very well.

The security forces are not entitled to the protection of a code of wartime morality in Ulster, because the British government has never accepted the IRA on its own definition, as an army, and has never declared a state of war in Northern Ireland. Instead, we have followed a policy of criminalization. The IRA are not accorded the status of an army. They have been categorized as terrorist criminals, who must be caught, convicted and sentenced for their crimes. Otherwise, normal conditions apply; and the security forces have no right to use force other than the necessary force to protect life.

Under these conditions, any police officer who chooses to apply wartime criteria in his analysis of what it is permissible to do, is out of step with official thinking. Could he be right in applying his own moral code whatever the official ruling? Possibly: after the example of the Third Reich we are all a little dubious about any absolutist claims for official morality, and private conscience has a high rating. However, it is significant that morally exemplary people under the Third Reich were usually reckoned as those who stood up and suffered for their beliefs by refusing to accept conventional state morality, such as Pastor Bonhoeffer; or who attempted to bring a corrupt and evil regime to an end by a single act of violence, such as Colonel von Stauffenberg. A police officer who went on a private campaign of violence to end the IRA's activities in Northern Ireland would correspond with neither example; and those who have tried have proved mentally ill rather than operating on a higher plane of personal morality. The morality of the policy of criminalization, I leave to be discussed by others.

It is a footnote worthy of sustained attention, that while the 43 police forces of England and Wales have yet to agree on an ethical code, either in concept or reality, the RUC created and launched its own code of Professional Policing Ethics some ten years ago, and that this code is the basis of police training from the very first day of recruit induction. The code consists of 12 principles, clearly defined and well brought to life. It is written in vigorous English and reads as neither pious nor patronizing. If you are interested in looking at an ethical code in use, read it.

THE LIMITATIONS OF AN ETHICAL CODE

An ethical code gives you a principle or formula to apply. It does not give you intellectual insight, nor moral courage, and it may not resolve all dilemmas. Ethics is not for children, as Aristotle said: and some moral dilemmas must be ended by a forced choice for the lesser of two evils. The practitioner may face a clash between official and personal morality, which the code does not resolve. A code does not provide integrity, but it helps its development.

CONCLUSION

Drawing up an ethical code is an exercise in applying moral philosophy. Endorsing it is simple enough. Making it something of everyday practical use is more difficult, partly because of the way in which police work is traditionally organized and carried out, and partly because we do not train people in general – let alone police officers – in how to think analytically in the first place. That is why our next chapter is on logic.

ANNEX

Declaration on the police. Council of Europe, 1979. Ethics

1. A police officer shall fulfil the duties the law imposes upon him by protecting his fellow citizens and the community against violent, predatory and other harmful acts, as defined by law.
2. A police officer shall act with integrity, impartiality and dignity. In particular he shall refrain from and vigorously oppose all acts of corruption.
3. Summary executions, torture and other forms of inhuman or degrading treatment or punishment remain prohibited in all circumstances. A police officer is under an obligation to disobey or disregard any order or instruction involving such measures.
4. A police officer shall carry out orders properly issued by his hierarchical superior, but he shall refrain from carrying out any order he knows, or ought to know, is unlawful.
5. A police officer must oppose violations of the law. If immediate or irreparable and serious harm should result from permitting the violation to take place he shall take immediate action, to the best of his ability.
6. If no immediate or irreparable and serious harm is threatened, he

must endeavour to avert the consequences of this violation, or its repetition, by reporting the matter to his superiors. If no results are obtained in that way he may report to higher authority.

7. No criminal or disciplinary action shall be taken against a police officer who has refused to carry out an unlawful order.

8. A police officer shall not cooperate in the tracing, arresting, guarding or conveying of persons who, while not being suspected of having committed an illegal act, are searched for, detained or prosecuted because of their race, religion or political belief.

9. A police officer shall be personally liable for his own acts and for acts of commission or omission he has ordered and which are unlawful.

10. There shall be a clear chain of command. It should always be possible to determine which superior may be ultimately responsible for acts or omissions of a police officer.

11. Legislation must provide for a system of legal guarantees and remedies against any damage resulting from police activities.

12. In performing his duties, a police officer shall use all necessary determination to achieve an aim which is legally required or allowed, but he may never use more force than is reasonable.

13. Police officers shall receive clear and precise instructions as to the manner and circumstances in which they should make use of arms.

14. A police officer having the custody of a person needing medical attention shall secure such attention by medical personnel and, if necessary, take measures for the preservation of the life and health of this person. He shall follow the instructions of doctors and other competent medical workers when they place a detainee under medical care.

15. A police officer shall keep secret all matters of a confidential nature coming to his attention, unless the performance of duty or legal provisions require otherwise.

16. A police officer who complies with the provisions of this declaration is entitled to the active moral and physical support of the community he is serving.

6
LOGIC AND ITS USES

Treason can never prosper. What's the reason?
For if it prosper, none dare call it treason!
Sir John Harington, Epigrams 1618

To attack logic is like driving to a meeting to protest the proliferation of road traffic. You have already conceded the usefulness of what you seek to oppose. I must use logic to explain logic. Is logic necessary? Logically, yes! Logic is a necessary but not a sufficient means to help make defendable moral decisions. A proper logical construction does not necessarily prove a moral argument to be correct. However, an illogical construction does show a moral argument to be invalid.

In what follows, I shall explain the basic tenets of logic. if you already know all this, then please fast forward. If you're not quite sure, then read on. In either case, you might consider the logical puzzles and their resolutions.

What is logic? Logic concerns consistency. A logical argument is one which is valid: ie, in which the conclusion follows from the premises. It is not necessarily true.

SYLLOGISM

That statement needs to be refined a little, but first we need to lay out the syllogism. The syllogism is the standard logical framework, and is the basis for argument. Argument does not mean a hot-headed confrontation, but an exposition of one's views in regard to a particular topic. If a logical framework is followed, then one's views are then open to analysis and refutation – or agreement. If not ...

'Do you believe in God?'
'Yes, I do.'
'Why?'

'Because I do.'
('So far, we have not reached an argument. All we have is an assertion.')
'Why do you believe in Him?'

At this point, the person being questioned has a choice. There are a number of arguments for the existence of God which are already reasonably well known, since this is an important topic and one which has been frequently debated. Equally, there are a number of well-known refutations for those arguments. The two disputants can now, if they are familiar with the standard arguments, move into a sort of theological chess, wherein one person puts forward arguments for the existence of God, and the other, if he so wishes, counters them. Since there is no irrefutable argument for the existence of God, this exercise, or game, will finally reach a stalemate. However, the better logician will have an advantage – provided that the other accepts the rules.

In this case, this may seem a rather sterile proceeding. If logic cannot help us decide the rather important question of whether or not God exists, then of what real use is it? Here I repeat my previous assertion: logic is a necessary but not a sufficient means towards clearer thought. It cannot give us our values, but it can help us apply them.

The framework of a syllogism

A syllogism consists of three parts:
   The general premiss, or law; the particular premiss, or observation; and the conclusion. The following examples are for reference.

First Example

General law	All gypsies are thieves
Observation	'Romany' Smith is a gypsy
Conclusion	'Romany' Smith is a thief.

This is an example of a valid deductive argument, or syllogism. It is normally expressed in algebraic terms, thus:

All As are Bs
C is an A
Therefore C is a B.

It is valid because the conclusion follows deductively from the premises. Is it true? No. Or rather, not necessarily. Romany Smith may be a thief: but the general law which premisses this argument is that all gypsies are thieves, and that cannot be true, since one counter-example is enough to disprove it. Therefore, although this is a valid syllogism, it is not true. If the general law were true, the observation were appropriate, and the conclusion followed deductively from the premisses, then the conclusion would also be true. However, not many real-life generalizations have such certainty, about people at any rate.

Second example
General law	All men are mortal
Observation	John Major is a man
Conclusion	Therefore, John Major is mortal.

At first sight this appears a better argument, both for its validity and truth. The only problem is the status of the general law. A law should be a useful empirical generalization, the knowledge of which enlarges our understanding of the world and helps us predict it better. But the statement 'all men are mortal' could also be seen as a definitional truth. It is part of our understanding of what makes a man, that he is mortal.

Knowledge check

It is worth your working through the following cases to make sure that you have grasped what this topic is about. Generally, but not always, logic and common sense concur!

1. All gypsies are thieves
'Romany' Smith is a thief
'Romany' Smith is a gypsy.
A. Is this conclusion valid or invalid?
B. is it true or false?
2. All gypsies are thieves
James is not a thief
Therefore, James is not a gypsy.
3. All triangles have three sides
This is a triangle
Therefore, it has three sides.
4. All tramps are vagabonds
James is a tramp
Therefore, James is a vagabond.
5. Some gypsies are thieves

Marcus is a gypsy
Therefore, Marcus may be a thief.
6. Some gypsies are thieves
Marcus is not a thief.
Therefore, Marcus cannot be a gypsy.

Commentary

1. The conclusion is neither valid nor true. The conclusion does not
    follow from the premisses. Technically, there is an undistributed
    middle term. In common sense terms, there are obviously many
    thieves who have no connections with gypsies.
2. Valid but untrue.
3. This syllogism is both valid and true, but does not get us very far.
    That is because, like many real-life statements, it is a definitional
    truth masquerading as an empirical one. It is part of the definition
    of a triangle that it has three sides. Rather than advancing our
    knowledge of the world, this argument repeats it. It is tautological
    rather than logical.
4. Like 3, this syllogism is both valid and true, but does not get us
    very far. Why not? Because 'tramp' and 'vagabond' are synonyms,
    and we have not really advanced our knowledge very far by
    substituting one roughly similar word for another.
5. Valid. True if the minor premiss is true. Some gypsies, like
    members of any other group, are thieves. If Marcus is a gypsy, he
    may be a thief. The conclusion is probabilistic rather than certain.
    This is an inductive syllogism, in which we cannot deduce but only
    infer the conclusion from the premisses. Most of the syllogisms we
    find useful in everyday life are like this, since there are very few
    generalizations we can make without exception.
6. Invalid and untrue.

Comment: logic, discrimination and prejudice

I have worked upon the example of the gypsy because it illustrates both
the usefulness and difficulty of using logic in a potentially contentious
occupation such as policing, in which to be consistent in one's attitudes
and behaviour may be far from enough. Few police officers would be so
naive, I suspect, as to state in an attributable context that because

someone is known to be a gypsy, that is sufficient cause to know him to be a thief. To make such a statement officially would be to give a hostage to fortune. However, in police folklore it is generally accepted that gypsies *are* thieves.

What are the implications of this sort of statement? Can it be justified empirically? Can it be justified morally? An activity will highlight the ethical issues.

ACTIVITY

You are the police commander in a troubled urban area with a rich proportion of immigrants in its population, where the police are under intense pressure from the community in general to enforce the law and protect the public to the greatest extent that your limited resources will allow. As a consenting police officer, you want local police policy and actions to reflect what the community wants. That means analysing local patterns of crime, disorder, vandalism and nuisance, and deciding where you can most effectively commit your resources.

The immigrants in your area come from a wide variety of origins, but there is one group – let us call them the Banshees – who are popularly or unpopularly believed to be disproportionately involved in a particular type of crime which is a great source of public disquiet.

So much for belief. When you examine all the evidence you can obtain, as objectively as possible, considering counter-hypotheses, assumptions, self-fulfilling prophecies and the like, the evidence strongly suggests that the popular assumption about the Banshees is correct. For whatever reason, they are disproportionately involved in crime x. It is now time to consider what you are going to do about it.

Background information

You know, as does everyone else, that Banshees, for historical reasons, are deeply suspicious of the police. They see the police as prejudiced against Banshees. Few Banshees join the police, and those that do are ostracized to the extent that they can only patrol in a Banshee area with difficulty. Many Banshee are highly politicized and very much aware of their 'rights'. If they suspect that the police are targeting them, for any reason, then they will make hay out of it. What are you going to do?

If you decide to mount a campaign against crime x –

1. To what extent are you going to target your activities, and on whom?
2. How will you declare that policy?
3. How will you justify it, and to whom?
4. What can you do to ensure that your activities are understood and supported, or at least not condemned out of hand, by at least a section of the group which, as a whole, is disproportionately connected with crime x?

Comment

This analysis could be applied to police activities against any recognizable group, even, for example, police operations against a group such as football supporters, who do not generally tend to attract the sympathy and support either of the public in general, or of those sections of it personally or professionally interested in the police misuse of power.

It may be that the working police officer will say that he is not responsible for the historical relationship that exists between police (and probably the state as a whole) and the Banshees; that he did not invent the statistics upon which police policies must be based; that the needs of the public in general must be considered, and not simply those of a minority who can shout loudly; that the police have a duty to uphold the law fairly, neutrally and impartially, and that this is what they are doing; and any number of other statements which may be both comforting and at least partially true (or do I mean valid?) from the police point of view.

That, however, is not enough. A police commander operates in a political context, in which it is insufficient to be able to decide what is the right thing to do, or even to be able to act consistently and according to a logical policy. The logic has to be shared.

···

COMMON LOGICAL ERRORS AND FALLACIES

Argument from authority

Who are you, to question my authority? I tell you that I am right.

In some cases, we are perfectly justified to argue from authority. Someone who has acquired a proper expertise in a particular area is entitled to air it – although he should still be subjected to critical questioning. However, an expertise in subject A does not make him an expert on B as well, and in a modern society it is generally considered inappropriate to accept anyone as an authority on a subject simply by virtue of his general status or power. Some people are clearly wiser than others, but that is another matter.

Argument ad hominem

That must be wrong, because Joe said it.

Put as crudely as this, this statement is obviously illogical – unless we can show that Joe is a thoroughly unreliable commentator in any context. However, arguments *ad hominem* are often disguised as something else, and need to be unpacked from their protective wrapping.

Who said that? Joe? Are you really going to believe him? Look what he said last week!

Literature is full of examples of prophets and soothsayers who have been considered mad, eccentric, or simply unreliable, only to be ignored by the audience at the very moment when they should have been given total attention and credence. There is no easy answer to this. It may be legitimate to argue against the man, but it is often a rhetorical ploy, rather than a valid logical stratagem.

The false analogy

This is when we draw a misleading comparison. For example, we may say that because someone has shown himself to be unfit to perform task X, so he will also be unfit to perform task Y. Since the two tasks may require different skills, the analogy may be false.

False analogies may be often found in areas such as selection, appraisal and promotion, where people are judged by irrelevant criteria. For example, it may be assumed that an indifferent constable would make a poor sergeant, whereas that may not necessarily be true. There are potentially justifiable reasons why we might not wish to promote an indifferent constable: but they should be justified by appropriate reasoning and not false analogy.

The unfalsifiable argument

Any empirical statement that we make, ie, any statement which attempts to expand our knowledge and understanding of the world, should be capable of being contradicted. Most statements about people are capable of being tested, at least in principle.

> A. *'I don't like Jews.'*
> B. 'Why not?'
> A. *'They're untrustworthy.'*
> B. '*All* of them are untrustworthy?'
> A. *'Yes. Every single one.'*
> B. 'What about Aaron Rosenberg?'
> A. *'That's different. He's....'*

And the speaker goes on to point to some reason why Aaron is the sole exception to his general law. The point is this: a general law becomes unfalsifiable at the point where, whatever counter-instance is put forward, the law is sustained, either by making exceptions, or by redefinition of the original statement. An argument *ad hominem* can be slipped in at this point, of course. Thus:

> B. Well, you would support the Jews, wouldn't you? Your sister married one.

There are clearly limits to the usefulness of logic, and a deep-seated prejudice cannot necessarily be removed simply by showing that it is illogical. As the Nazis said: 'Everyone knows one good Jew' – showing that their prejudice was so deep-seated that they could afford to acknowledge an apparent contradiction. Outside Nazi Germany, of course, anti-semitism may be concealed as something else, and not articulated in such a way that it can easily be challenged. The same applies to any prejudice. As human beings, we tend to generalize. It is how we make sense of the world. The difference between generalization and prejudice is that the generalizer is prepared to analyse and discuss the rationality of his generalizations, and recognizes when it is legitimate to generalize and when it is not.

'Cognitive dissonance reduction' is the clumsy phrase by which psychologists explain (or, to be more accurate, describe) how the mind can hold two contradictory theories simultaneously. We might more simply refer to rationalization. If we are comfortable with our stereotypes and generalizations, but do not necessarily wish to be thought of as bigoted, then the ability to rationalize both our own prejudices and others's objections to them is a great comforter. The clear thinker recognizes the difference between rationality and rationalization, in his own thoughts, as well as other peoples'!

Self-fulfilling prophecies

A self-fulfilling prophecy is a failure of evidence-gathering. Instead of going out to test our hypothesis against reality by finding evidence which goes against it, we look only for evidence that confirms it. This is called verification, and its opposite falsification, which we have already explored in the context of unfalsifiability.

As the philosopher and logician Karl Popper showed, verification can never prove a theory to be true, since there is always the possibility that the next instance will disconfirm it. Popper believes, therefore, that we can never establish absolute truth, but must merely propose and work with hypotheses which have so far proved more useful than others, ie, they have not yet been falsified. Popper's work is of considerable relevance to the process of criminal investigation, where an open mind is the senior detective's greatest asset. However, the convicted criminal cannot usually benefit from Popper's scheme. He is guilty: the Court has verified it!

Post hoc ergo propter hoc

Because A is followed by B, it does not follow that A caused B. The police may invest a large amount of time and money in a road safety campaign – probably, in these days of multi-agency approaches, to be pursued with other public agencies of local or national government. When the next official statistics are produced, lo and behold, fatal road deaths have gone down in number.

It is extremely tempting for any public service agency in this situation to claim the credit for what has occurred. However, unless it can be demonstrated that A (expenditure on a road safety campaign) causes B (an improvement in road safety, as measured by accurate and meaningful statistics) then it is a fallacy to claim that A has caused B, and any such inference may be a very dangerous one.

Circumstantial evidence

If X is seen leaving a public house in which Y has just been stabbed, it does not follow that X stabbed Y. As every trainee constable knows, circumstantial and direct evidence are not the same. It would be direct evidence that X stabbed Y if a witness, or better still a number of witnesses, could be produced who had seen the stabbing and were prepared to swear in court that X stabbed Y. Does that mean that circumstantial evidence is of no value? No, for an accumulation of circumstantial evidence may help to weight a case against someone. Suppose X, in addition to being seen leaving the public house just after Y was stabbed, had blood on his coat. Suppose he had been known to buy a large knife on the day of the stabbing. Suppose he were seen to drop something heavy into the local canal on his way home, and that a subsequent search produced the murder weapon. Suppose he had been known to have quarrelled bitterly with Y, in the recent past. And finally, suppose that when questioned by the police his manner was awkward and suspicious, and that he could account for none of the above events in such a way as to clear him from suspicion. None of these facts on its own is enough to put him in the dock, and all might have innocent explanations, or have no connection to the fatal event. Put together, however, they increase the probability that he is the guilty party. In logical terms, circumstantial evidence is inductive rather than deductive, and its wiles need to be understood.

The detective is logician, and the logician detective. Or is that a false analogy?

....

CASE STUDY

Everyday life is so full of illogic that one is tempted to suppose either that consistency is not a prized virtue for most people, or that Aristotle's syllogism can be used as an analytic tool only within the confines of a rather small group: ie, those who have read Aristotle and accept his framework. However, although we should not all know a syllogism if it bit us, illogical arguments are generally recognized as such, when people stop and think.

In a world in which more time is devoted to communicating than thinking, analysis is undervalued; fact and value or opinion are confused; and the supposed general laws underlying particular assertions are seldom exposed, let alone probed for their validity. Am I exaggerating things? Please read on.

The madness of pursuing sexual equality

Summarized in 'The Week', 30 November 1996, from the *Daily Mail*.

The pursuit of sexual equality is threatening to destroy our armed forces and essential services, says Leo McKinstry. In the warped world of political correctness, it is deemed more important to reflect the composition of our society than to protect it. Increasing numbers of women are being drafted into these jobs; but they require strength, and in this respect it is dangerous to pretend men and women are equal. Recently, a man had a heart attack. When the ambulance came, the two women paramedics could not carry him down the stairs. Had a neighbour not helped, he might have died.

We have had the finest armed forces, fire brigade and police in Europe precisely because they were dominated by the traditional male virtues of physical courage, toughness and resilience. The feminisation of these services is beginning to produce a quite different culture: the self-absorbed culture of complaint. Is it mere coincidence that we are beginning to hear demands from the police for compensation for stress and trauma which arise from their public duties?

Analysis

Destruction (line 1) is a very strong consequence to predict. Threatening to destroy is clever, because it reduces the testability of the argument. (This may not be why the author or summarizer used the phrase.)

So many implicit general laws underlie this short extract, that it is difficult to know where to begin. Here are some of its assumptions:

a. Men are generally stronger than women.
b. Strength is necessary for the tasks carried out by members of the armed forces and emergency services.
c. Women must therefore be at a disadvantage in carrying out those tasks.
d. (In addition) women do not share the traditional male virtues of physical courage, toughness and resilience.
e. Therefore, if they are recruited into the emergency services there will be a decline in those services' performance (irrespective of the strength of the people employed).
f. To enlist women in these organizations (in the interests of pursuing sexual equality) is therefore madness.

Comment

a. 'Generally'; that does not mean that no woman is suitable.

b. In some cases strength is indispensable. A firefighter needs considerable strength to carry other people up and down ladders. But do all members of the emergency services need that strength? It would be more accurate to say that strength is desirable rather than necessary.

c. Some women would be at a disadvantage in carrying out some tasks, yes.

d and e. The assumption seems overstated. In any case, it would be just as plausible to assume (in the absence of proof for either assertion) that the sort of woman who is going to join the emergency services in the face of traditionalist opposition, is either going to quickly prove wholly unsuitable (in which case she will be weeded out), or of above average acceptability. Few Roman Catholics join the RUC, but those who do join tend to do well, presumably because their determination and resilience is greater than average. The same assumption may hold for women.

It would be quite simple to test the decline in performance hypothesis, by noting how many female members of the essential services are reporting sick and/or claiming stress, compared with how many male practitioners. If the men are reporting sick because of the stress caused by working with women, what happened to the traditional male virtues of courage, toughness and resilience?

f. The conclusion does not follow as a deductive argument, and is debatable as a piece of inductive logic. Moreover, the assumption that the recruiting policy is based upon political correctness can be challenged. There are other reasons for recruiting from a broader basis than tradition would allow.

Review

Somewhere inside all this there is a strongly-felt argument struggling to emerge. The writer wishes to argue that women should not be allowed to join the essential services. There are plenty of ways to put this which do not rest upon pseudo-empirical and over-generalized foundations. For example, one might quote history, tradition, or some religious teachings. An anti-female policy might even be justified consequentially, if we could predict with any certainty what the future holds for us, and if our predictions did not affect the course of events by their very utterance. It is potentially relevant to the debate that men are generally stronger and physically tougher than women; that emergency work does require rough-and-ready strength; and that men need work. We are on dubious ground if we say that as the weaker sex, women need to be protected, if necessary, from themselves; but it can still be argued that the traditional division of labour between the sexes makes for a happier and more harmonious society, and that the concept of chivalry is a useful one; although how one could actually test this proposition is hard to say.

Finally, in a multi-cultural society, should we not be balancing the modern notion of sexual equality against more traditional views? Immigrants from traditional societies may be opposed to 'Western' notions of equality, and believe that a woman's place is in the home. If the police exist primarily to deal with society as it is, rather than as some would like it to be, and if it be easier to investigate and resolve crime and conflict within certain communities by using only male (or female) officers, then those are pragmatic grounds for doing so.

These arguments illustrate the complexities of any reality-based dispute, the need to analyse its logical foundations, and the need to make an objective scrutiny of the relevant information. You will have seen flaws in the alternative arguments I put forward, as to why we might discriminate against women in the emergency services. What is important is to debate the issues logically, comprehensively and fairly.

The following activity (in two parts) will allow you to do so.

....

....

ACTIVITY

1. There has been a murder within the Asian community which you
    police. Normally, you would simply have opened a box of
    detectives, and set them to work regardless of anything other
    than their professional ability and motivation. However, in this
    situation you have good reason to expect that female detectives,
    whether operating alone, with another female, or with a man, will
    find it difficult to be accepted as investigators. In other words, the
    efficiency of the enquiry is likely to be affected by an issue which
    would be largely irrelevant in another context.

    ☐ What are you going to do about it?

2. The notion of chivalry is being discarded by the criminal and anti-
    social element in your police area, and women police are as likely
    to be attacked as men. Whereas once you could have sent a woman
    officer to arrest a leading criminal, respond to an emergency, or
    clear a pub, reasonably secure in the knowledge that she would not
    be attacked, that assumption no longer holds. The women under
    your command are keen to prove their worth and are not asking for
    special favours. However, many of their male colleagues are far
    from happy about the situation, and disquiet has been expressed at
    community meetings about attacks on women officers.

    ☐ What are you going to do about it?

....

CONCLUSION

As I began by saying, logic is a necessary but not a sufficient means
towards better decisions. If we are to be understood in what we do we
must be clear and consistent in how we explain our actions. Clarity and
consistency may not be enough – but consider their alternatives.

7
CASE STUDIES

I believe the first test of a truly great man is his humility. I do not mean by humility, doubt of his own power, or hesitation of speaking his opinions; but a right understanding of the relation between what he can do and say, and the rest of the world's sayings and doings. All great men not only know their business, but usually know that they know it; and are not only right in their main opinions, but they usually know that they are right in them; and they do not think much of themselves on that account. Arnolfo knows he can build a good dome at Florence; Albert Durer writes calmly to one who has found fault with his work – 'it cannot be better done'; Sir Isaac Newton knows he has worked out a problem or two that would have puzzled anybody else; only they do not expect their fellow men to fall down, therefore, and worship them. They have a curious under-sense of powerlessness, knowing that the greatness is not in them, but through them – that they could not do or be anything else than God made them; and they see something divine and God-made in every other man they meet, and are endlessly, foolishly, incredibly merciful.

John Ruskin, *Frondes Agrestes*, 1901

(And yet) when I looked upon that ugly idol in the glass, I was conscious of no repugnance, rather a leap of welcome. This, too, was myself. It seemed natural and human. In my eyes it bore a livelier image of the spirit, it seemed more express and single, than the imperfect and divided countenance I had hitherto been accustomed to call mine. And in so far I was doubtless right. I have observed that when I bore the semblance of Edward Hyde, none could come near me at first without a visible misgiving of the flesh. This, as I take it, was because all human beings as we meet them, are commingled out of good and evil: and Edward Hyde, alone in the ranks of man, was pure evil.

Robert Louis Stevenson, *Dr Jekyll and Mr Hyde*, 1994

CASE STUDIES AND OTHER PRACTICAL METHODS FOR EXPLORING MORAL DILEMMAS

Usefulness

Case studies are strongly attacked as a teaching method by the influential North American writer on police ethics, Edwin Delattre. His argument is as follows:

☐ Most case studies are dreamed up by academics, who have no real understanding of police dilemmas. Their problems tend to be over-sophisticated and complex, whereas real-life ethical dilemmas are generally simple, stark choices between good and evil.

☐ In any case, police officers do not, as a priority, need training in sophisticated moral analysis. It is far more important that they be the right sort of people, than that they be intellectually capable of resolving hypothetical problems on paper – which they are unlikely to encounter in reality.

In Delattre's (1989) words:

Most of what matters in moral life does not involve difficult decisions. Our lives are not filled with the situations of the sort popular in ethics courses, such as what to do when not everyone can fit in the only available lifeboat. Giving such hypothetical problems the central place in ethics is highly misleading. Complicated hypothetical problems may refine our thinking, but only after we have given due importance to commonplace morality.

Few common moral failings and failures stem from inept reasoning about dilemmas. Many more arise from moral indifference, disregard for other people, weakness of will, and bad or self-indulgent habits.

I agree with Delattre that the problem solving approach is not enough, and that a competent hypothetical problem solver who does not put his theoretical values into practice because he lacks integrity is not a good police officer. Nevertheless, I feel that there is a strong argument for problem solving by case study in police ethical training, provided that:

☐ The training takes place in an atmosphere conducive to free and open debate.

☐ The tutor (who may or may not be a police officer) is ready and competent to raise the intellectual level by encouraging the group to analyse issues raised within a moral framework, in language with

....

which they feel comfortable. It may be necessary, in order to achieve this, to establish that police officers *do* face moral dilemmas, and what they consist of.

☐ Discussion and resolution of case studies leads to a frank and help-ful discussion of real-life examples of ethical dilemmas within the group, which are sparked off by the hypothetical cases considered.

A good police officer of any rank is someone who:

☐ Sets an example of good behaviour.
☐ Encourages debate on ethical dilemmas.
☐ Is open, positive and willing to learn, to share and to teach.

Any police officer may influence the behaviour of other officers, and in this area the unofficial group leader – the old sweat, who has seen it all before, and is likely to have acquired a thick and glistening patina of cynicism, like an old piece of furniture which has been polished many times as it is prepared for sale by its various owners – may have more influence on recruits and probationers than their official leaders, particularly if those official leaders are not much older than those whom they command.

Consequently, it would be wrong to suggest that there are certain responsibilities for police officers placed in official positions of leadership, which put them in a different category to the constables they command.

☐ All police officers contribute to setting the tone for the organization.
☐ All police officers face and make moral decisions, both for themselves and others.
☐ All police officers can influence their colleagues' behaviour.
☐ All officers, therefore, will benefit by developing their powers of ethical decision making.

If they are in positions of power, they will have greater opportunities to influence what happens. They will also need to set an example in a greater range of activities, since rank gives power and power can be misused, particularly if the senior officer's motives are assumed to be based on the interests of the organization, rather than his own wants. (Who questions the Chief Officer's need to use a helicopter, rather than other transport?)

CASE STUDIES AND HYPOTHETICALS

These are very similar. The distinction I would draw is that a case study is offered complete from the outset, whereas a hypothetical can be developed by the investigator in response to the immediate reaction of the person presented with the problem. (Socrates invented the method.) Most of the examples that follow are case studies. We begin with a hypothetical.

Method
1. The investigator begins by describing a situation and posing a dilemma to a group.
2. The investigator asks someone to offer a solution to the dilemma, as it has been posed so far.
3. A response is offered.
4. The investigator then analyses what the person has said, and either puts further points to him, or offers the problem, as it has developed, to someone else.
5. The process continues until sufficient learning has been gained from that scenario.
6. The investigator may choose to indicate what he thinks were the general points arising from the scenario, in regard to ethical principles. Alternatively, he may ask the group to identify them.
7. A discussion follows.

In pedagogical jargon, this has been a 'learning event', and every learning event deserves a debrief.

A simple scenario

The problem

Your colleague James Wellbeloved is off sick. That evening you are watching the highlights of the day's racing on television. The roving camera picks out James – large, jolly, excited and apparently bursting with health and exuberance – watching the horses being paraded around the small ring before one of the races.

You sit back in astonishment. What is James doing there, when he had reported sick? And perhaps more importantly, what are you going to do about it?

Once you have stated the problem to your chosen group, you should allow them time to ponder, and then ask someone to state his view. You can then either probe immediately, or go on to others to see if and how their opinions differ, before you home in on someone to explore deeper.

Initial options and possible probes

The broad alternatives open at this stage appear to do nothing, or to take action. Let us explore them in turn, with the investigator's possible options for exploration in italics.

To do nothing
Why not?
    a. The episode is trivial.
In itself, possibly. But someone is acting deceitfully – or appears to be doing so. Moreover, there could be other matters arising from this. For example, is the supposedly sick person failing to produce important work? Or putting more work on other people?
    b. We've all done it.
Again, possibly true – in some form or another. But is that a good reason to ignore this episode?
    c. The evidence was obtained accidentally.
So is a lot of evidence. Does that mean that it is unfair to use it? Would you never use evidence that was obtained accidentally?
    d. The evidence could be misleading.
Certainly. But that could be a reason to investigate further, rather than ignore the episode. You may dismiss something as unproven, but in reality not forget it at all. That could mean that you retain a lingering doubt about a colleague's truthfulness or reliability, which may be unfounded.
    e. The cure may be worse than the disease.
In a sense, yes. Investigating a relatively trivial episode may give rise to serious consequences. But that is an argument for a careful investigation – not for none.

To take action

☐ *What sort of action?*
☐ *How far are you going to push this?*
☐ *Who else may you involve?*
☐ *What are your legal and managerial responsibilities, and how do they compare with your ethical promptings?*

Variations
The investigator could introduce uncertainty.

☐ *What action would you have taken, if you were not really sure that it was James?*
☐ *What if you confront him, and he disputes the facts and claims that he was at home? Are you going to make a police investigation out of this, and look for evidence to support or deny his alibi? Or are you going to accept his word that you may have been mistaken? Would you feel, deep down, quite pleased if he denied it, because you felt that it absolved you from further responsibility? Or would you feel inclined to press harder?*

Another way to vary the problem is to introduce further information, either *ab initio*, or as a solution is developed. For example, the investigator could develop the relationship between the witness and the apparent offender.

Varying the relationship

☐ James is a close colleague.
☐ James is a subordinate in the same department.
☐ James is a subordinate in another department.
☐ James is senior, in the same department or elsewhere.
☐ James is a civilian employee of the police service.

Reactions
All these variations, which can be otherwise combined, may lead to differing initial reactions to the problem.
   Oh, well! If he's only a civilian....

And underlying issues

However, I would suggest that as the analysis goes deeper and fundamental factors are identified for discussion, so apparent differences will seem less important.
   So civilians are allowed to make false claims, are they? And that doesn't affect anyone else?

Mitigating circumstances

These are easily invented. For example:

....

☐ James is known to have been working extremely hard recently. If anyone deserves a day at the races, he does. In any case, if he had claimed for the overtime for which he is due, the organization would owe him a great deal of money.

☐ James has been under a lot of strain recently.

Analysis

What are the underlying principles in this case? I would suggest four: justice, fairness, a sense of proportion – and compassion.

Universal questions

Whatever stage of the scenario has been reached and whatever variations introduced, I would suggest that the following questions could always be asked of any proposed course of action or inaction:

☐ *Is it (what you are proposing) fair?*
☐ *Is it reasonable?*
☐ *Is it the utmost you can do, in the circumstances?*
☐ *Is it a solution with which you would be happy to live, in the long term?*

CASES

The studies which follow are intended to be fictional but realistic. They do not necessarily relate to the United Kingdom, and are not necessarily set in the present. You will need to suspend your disbelief in any details which would not ring true in your force, and not answer each dilemma from the perspective of what regulations may or may not say. Dilemmas are about choice. Since you will probably be reading this book on your own, you will first address the cases for yourself. If you are able to discuss them with colleagues, or put them on the agenda in a formal or informal teaching environment, then you will gain other things from the experience. We tend to assume that other people recognize the same moral dilemmas as we do, share the same problem-solving techniques, and operate from the same values. Even if we practise the same profession, none of these assumptions is necessarily true. Honest and open discussion of moral dilemmas by members of a peer group who wish to learn from each other is a rich diet – although it can lead to indigestion.

. . . .

Order

As in real life, these cases are in random order. Some relate to personal issues, some more to professional problems. You will decide which are which, and which are more important.

Analysis

There are many ways to classify the analysis of ethical problems, according to the school of ethics to which you belong. I should like to compare three ethical approaches, and in doing so bring out some lessons about how to resolve ethical dilemmas in a sensible way. The chosen approaches are absolute, consequentialist and pragmatic. Scholars may dispute the distinctions between them. My objective will have been achieved if they prove both comprehensible and useful.

1. The absolute approach

The absolute position has the merit of simplicity. For instance, suppose that a watch has been stolen and the thief identified. The mental processes of pure absolutism would be:

> *This person has stolen a watch.*
> *Stealing is wrong.*
> *Therefore, the thief must be arrested, charged, convicted and punished.*

Are there any mitigating circumstances?

These do not concern the absolutist. Whatever is stolen, and for whatever reason, stealing is wrong.

— Will the punishment correct the thief's behaviour?
— Will it deter others from carrying out acts of theft?
— Will it act as a warning to society?

Those are not absolutist concerns. Punishment is punishment. A true absolutist would still punish a person, even if it could be accurately foretold that the punishment would serve to harden the wrong-doer in his iniquity. The absolutist is concerned with the perpetrator of the crime, and what happens to him. The effect upon society is of less concern. The absolutist may argue that it is important that society show its abhorrence for a crime, by its emphatic denunciation: but again, that would be because it is the right thing to do, rather than for its effect.

Would an absolutist bend the rules? Would he shade the evidence so that a probably guilty person was convicted, even if the formal evidence were incomplete? Psychologically, he might. Logically, this would be contradictory. Absolutism is absolute. If we apply it to process, and the rules say that the rules must never be bent, then it would be absolutely wrong to bend them.

Comment

☐ The absolutist may be disposed to equate crime with sin.
☐ Absolutism and fundamentalism are related.
☐ There are occasions when we may all be absolutists, and wish to emphatically condemn something and punish its practitioners, simply because we believe it to be wrong. Some crimes, for example crimes against children, arouse an almost universal condemnation. Indeed, even the perpetrators of such crimes may condemn them.

I couldn't help it, Doctor. It was my nerves.

However, pure absolutism is unworkable as a general ethical principle, and would prove wholly dysfunctional for police officers.

Why is absolutism unworkable?

An absolutist police officer would be unable to exercise discretion as to whether or not to enforce the law, and which law to enforce where he had a choice. He would be unable to balance public tranquillity against law enforcement, as Lord Scarman put it. In other words, he would be unable to police intelligently, by consent.

Secondly, a police officer has to be able to change his priorities as circumstances change. There is little point in working yourself up into a paroxysm of righteous fervour about child abuse or attacks on old people, if next week you are to be posted to traffic. Indeed, it may be, as we have said elsewhere in this book, that a police officer is better suited to his work if he is *not* motivated by constant moral outrage. It is better to be an objectively minded professional investigator who wants to find out the facts, than a zealot who has already decided who is guilty.

Finally, few police officers will have the luxury of deciding whether or not to investigate a particular crime, in isolation. They will usually face competing priorities, in which to investigate X must mean to neglect Y. In a situation of shifting knowledge, simple absolute judgements may be hard to make.

Any police officer needs a clear set of values, and those values should include knowing when to stop, withdraw, or let go, and how to cope with the frustration that this causes. Police work *is* frustrating, if you are a crusader for justice; and the police officer must be able to live with this, while retaining his enthusiasm and not becoming cynical. A tall order, but not impossible.

Relativism: a false path

The apparent opposite of absolutism is relativism; but that is not the basis for a moral philosophy. A pure relativist, who bases his conduct upon the notion that all moral standards are relative, might be able to avoid causing offence in the short term, while people admire his broadmindedness and disinclination to condemn. Counsellors such as Carl Rogers have elevated tolerance and non-commitment into primary virtues; but in the end, most people want to know what the other person thinks of them, and their conduct.

Do you think that what I did was right or wrong?
What else could I have done?
What would you have done?

2. The consequentialist approach

The consequentialist is the opposite of the absolutist, in that before a person takes action he wishes to calculate its consequences.

Suppose, as before, that a watch has been stolen and the thief identified.

The consequentialist will want to know far more than the absolutist, before he decides upon the appropriate response to this event. For example:

- ☐ Was the watch valuable, either financially or sentimentally?
- ☐ Will the owner regret its loss?
- ☐ How difficult will it be to convict the offender?
- ☐ Does the offender have a violent or otherwise anti-social history?
- ☐ What will the whole investigation cost?

Rather than decide matters on a simple yes/no moral basis, the consequentialist will attempt to envisage the likely consequences of his possible options for action, and their comparative acceptability. In some cases, this is a relatively simple and uncontroversial exercise. For example, suppose that the stolen watch is of insignificant value.

The owner has no regrets as to its loss. The thief has no criminal record. The cost of a formal prosecution would vastly outweigh its apparent value. In such circumstances, few would argue for a prosecution, and a formal caution would be the recommended policy. If there is no initial lead as to the identity of the thief upon which to base any investigation, then to use police jargon, the crime will be screened out from the start: in other words, it will be bottom of the list of priorities for police action. Crime screening and graded response are consequentialist policies. (For any readers not familiar with the logic and operation of these policies, they are explored in Villiers, 1995, Chapter 10.)

On the other hand, suppose the watch is of sentimental value, and the owner grievously upset by its theft, particularly as violence was threatened (but not used) to steal it. However, the identification of the thief is insecure. Further evidence is needed but unlikely to appear, and a prosecution would be of uncertain success.

What should the good police officer do? Devote scarce resources to the increasingly elusive search for evidence? Anticipate the probable advice of the police hierarchy (with the Crown Prosecution Service in mind) that this case cannot merit further effort, and close down the investigation? Find some other way of reassuring and protecting the victim, other than by convicting the thief?

As soon as we begin to analyse this example, we see that absolute and consequential strands of thought are interwoven. In deciding upon the proper course of action we are always making a moral judgement, even if we do not call it so; and consequences, where they can be foretold, must be evaluated as good or bad. How are we to do that? The usual method is to apply the logic of utilitarianism.

Utilitarianism

To be classificatory for a moment (and I promise never to do it again) utilitarianism is a sub-set of consequentialism. In other words, a utilitarian argument is also consequentialist: but a consequentialist argument is not necessarily utilitarian. All clear? Then we can get on!

Utilitarianism is the brand of thought developed by the philosopher, would-be legal reformer and animal rights enthusiast Jeremy Bentham (1748–1832) and by his followers James Mill and his son John Stuart Mill (who later moved away from it). Bentham said that in any choice we should choose the option which will have the greatest utility: in other words, which will increase the greatest happiness of the greatest number. People's happiness is to count equally: each person is to count for one, and none for more than one. Happiness is quantifiable, and there is no difference in quality between forms of happiness. What does this imply? Here is a contemporary example. Suppose Bentham were alive today, and chairman of the board which distributes the charitable levy of the National Lottery. To whom should this levy be given? Bentham would argue, presumably, that opera and ballet should receive very little money, since they are arcane pursuits which do not appeal to large numbers. They cannot be said to be superior in quality or cultural value to any other activity, since such a distinction cannot be made in Bentham's schema. The counter-argument that opera, ballet and such-like activities are superior and deserve to be subsidized is an absolutist one. In fact, lobbyists who want the higher culture to be subsidized do not tend to refer to it as an elitist activity, but rather as one which large numbers of people would enjoy if only they were to try it. And, of course, they can only try it if the price is subsidized.... I think we can guess what Bentham would say to that. There is nonsense, and there is nonsense on stilts! The consumer is the best judge of his happiness, and not the state on his behalf.

If we consider police activities, then the utilitarian calculation can be an extremely helpful one, and is much used. Lord Scarman uses a utilitarian rationale when he argues a police officer should use his discretion to ensure public tranquillity, rather than simply to enforce the law whatever the cost. After all, the greatest happiness of the greatest number will be better served by the absence of a major riot, than by the possible conviction of one petty offender. In the case studies which follow, the principle of utility can often be applied. The learning will be in the detail. In the meantime, let us consider some of the possible drawbacks of consequentialism as a general approach.

Problems with the consequentialist approach

The consequentialist approach can raise problems. First, we have to ask: consequences for whom? In the case of the watch, we have a variety of contenders. If we apply the principle of utility, then we are asserting that we can know which course of action will lead to the greatest happiness of the greatest number. In some cases, it may be possible to argue a case which reasonable people would generally accept, as to which course of action will serve that result. In other cases, it may be impossible to frame such an argument.

Incomplete knowledge

We may not know enough, even in the present, to be able to say which option will suit more people.

Difficulties with prediction

We may have difficulties with the time-frame. After all, it is relatively easy to consider the immediate consequences of an act, but much more difficult to know its long-term impact. The philosopher Karl Popper (1902–1996) asserted that every act has unintended consequences, and that therefore the purpose of social engineering should be to remove obvious and generally agreed faults, rather than attempt to create a utopian society which will have defects which could not have been anticipated (Magee, 1968). The work of other theorists, from Heisenberg (1901–1976) with his famous indeterminacy principle as discovered in 1925, to those who advance chaos theory (I cannot bring myself to coin the neologism 'chaoists'), supports Popper's view.

Personal values

Although the consequentialist sets his argument within a supposedly objective framework, there is still an irremovable element of personal judgement. The police officer, as any other public official, will use his own beliefs, values and prejudices to decide the suitability of a proposed course of action.

Playing God

The absolutist is liable to be accused of playing God, since his actions in condemning wrong-doing are explicitly judgemental. However, in attempting to know the future the consequentialist is also playing at God.

3. The pragmatic approach

A man steals a watch, and the owner reports its theft to the police. The pragmatist will ask:

- [ ] Of what value was the watch to its owner, both in financial and sentimental terms?
- [ ] What would be the cost of investigating this crime?
- [ ] What is the likelihood of success?
- [ ] What are the opportunity costs of investigating this crime? In other words, what resources would it distract from elsewhere?

☐ How does investigating this crime rate against the priorities for police activity, which have been decided at a local, county and national level?

☐ How else might the crime be investigated, other than by a full-scale CID investigation?

So far the pragmatist has made much the same appraisal as a consequentialist. What distinguishes the two, *inter alia*, is that the pragmatist does not attempt to know the unknowable – what will happen in the future. What does he do?

First, by evaluating and reconciling such potentially competing priorities as value, moral outrage, public interest, use of scarce resources, and the likelihood of success, the pragmatist decides upon the right initial course of action in this case.

Secondly, he applies a system which allows for concurrent activity and continuing evaluation. As a good pragmatist, he will review progress in the light of emerging information, so that he might close down one inquiry which had begun promisingly, or revive another in the light of fresh evidence.

Thirdly, the good police pragmatist knows the importance of routine. Many police activities are worth carrying out, not because they will necessarily produce results in a particular case, but as a necessary part of an efficient organization's approach to its duties.

The importance of routine

In our rather overworked example, the stolen watch is described and the description both circulated and retained. These are normal police activities, and should be carried out efficiently and effectively. In due course, it may be that when the activities and possessions of a receiver of stolen property are investigated, the watch will be found and identified, together with other items. The thief will be prosecuted, and the timepiece restored to its owner. On the other hand, the watch may never be heard of again. The good pragmatist knows that his system is self-maintaining and can cope with either eventuality.

Let us consider another example. A woman is murdered, and the body found by her milkman. There are no obvious leads as to the murderer. What would the pragmatist do? First, he would instigate a full-scale murder inquiry. Is that a pragmatic decision? Yes – because it is laid down for him. No murder goes uninvestigated. Does he continue with a full-scale investigation until the crime is solved? The answer is no, he cannot. Murder is the most serious crime, and therefore cannot go ignored; but nor can it be allowed to consume resources *ad infinitum*. At some point the officer in charge of the investigation has to decide when to stop it. Pragmatically, he will consider factors such as the state of public opinion in regard to the crime; the likelihood of fresh evidence emerging at this stage; the cost of the investigation to date; and the other demands upon his resources.

If he decides to cease full-time investigation, that should not mean that the case is closed. Although the murder has not been solved, the descriptions of the people who have been identified as suspects are kept on file, and forensic evidence is stored for future use. A few years later there is another murder in a different county, wherein the murderer shows a strikingly similar *modus operandi*. The description of the second murderer matches one of our five suspects for the first case, and because of the existence of accurate and extensive records, which have been kept as a matter of (pragmatic) routine, both crimes are resolved.

Is pragmatism a moral option?

Yes. It is sensible to make good use of police resources. Devoting major resources to the investigation of a crime which is unlikely to be solved, and while there are competing priorities, is not ethically justifiable. Professional skill and judgement are vital for successful pragmatism. Pragmatic ethics means weighing up the factors, and making a robust and defendable decision.

Conclusion

In conclusion, there is no one right way to analyse moral dilemmas, and there may be situations when, as the British General Macready remarked in Ireland in 1921: 'Whatever we do, we shall be bound to be wrong.' (He had refused joint command of the army and the police, and that was certainly the wrong decision.) No single ethical problem-solving technique may have all the answers, but its use will raise the quality of debate.

BACK TO SCHOOL

Your force believes it both right and proper to be actively involved in helping develop good citizenship in schools, and it has a number of carefully selected and specially trained schools liaison officers, who visit the schools in the force area and, in coordination with the normal teachers, take part in the school programme. The police officers are expected to build a rapport with both pupils and staff, and their contribution is very broad, ranging from giving advice on practical safety measures to education in good citizenship. It is an acknowledged aim of the programme to present the police in a positive light, and encourage children to see them as not simply an agency of enforcement and repression, but as an organization which needs the active cooperation of the public to fulfil its aim of policing by consent.

One of your officers comes to you with a problem. He became a school liaison officer and is finding the work both satisfying and worthwhile. However, he is now finding himself under increasing pressure from the drugs squad to provide information on school-children who may be actively involved in drug-dealing, and their contacts.

Should he go along with this policy? He feels some qualms about this, and is not sure of the rights and wrongs of the situation. Is it ethical? What should he do?

Analysis

The school liaison officer needs to be clear on his duties as a police officer, and the contract under which he is employed. It would seem sensible to emphasize that he is an open and declared police officer, who has a duty to investigate crime if it comes to his attention. However, his role in the school is primarily educational, rather than investigative, and he should not set out to deceive. He is certainly not there simply to encourage pupils to become juvenile informants – the employment of whom raises particular moral dilemmas in any case, and for which he has not been trained.

In other words, his real and declared positions should be the same, unless a difference can be justified by standard moral criteria in cases of deception. If he is to set out to deceive, and this policy can be justified, then it must have been justified to him before he accepted the job.

. . . .

On a practical note, risk analysis applies here. Most deceptions are discovered. Is it worth compromising the reputation for integrity of the police with an entire generation of school-children, whatever the supposed gains?

CHOICE

A police officer junior to you approaches you and asks to join your department.

She is young, keen, full of ideas and extremely hard working, and you would love to have her join. She claims that her present boss is a dinosaur and that if she has to remain where she is she will think very seriously of leaving the police service.

You know her boss, a severe, old-fashioned, righteous disciplinarian whose department faces many problems. You are colleagues but not friends. Officially, you cannot arrange the request for transfer. There is a cumbersome and highly bureaucratic process of interdepartmental transfer, which is unlikely to work in your favour. Unofficially, you could have this officer moved fairly easily.

☐ What will you do?
☐ What implications might your decision have for the organization?
☐ What are the underlying ethical issues?

Analysis

There is a conflict of duty here, and you have to contrast the needs of the individual with the needs of the organization. To act expediently may be extremely tempting. After all, this appears a one-off case; it need not set a precedent, and there is much to be gained. On the other hand, to poach the would-be mover is probably not a solution you would recommend to others. You will not be able to keep it quiet. And it will create a climate of ambiguity within your organization. Do we follow the rules, or not?

Police experience may already have caused you to consider the motives of the officer who wants a transfer, in coming to you in the first place. Will she do the same thing again, when she meets another problem? And is that your concern?

Lateral thinking may suggest another solution to the problem, which is able to reconcile apparent contradictions. Whether or not that is possible, this is a clear example of a case where one should consider the long-term consequences of one's actions.

....

CORRUPTION

You are a police officer working as head of CID in a developing country, under contract to the Overseas Development Agency, a section of the Foreign Office which posts police officers abroad. You intend to return to British policing in the long-term, and hope to reach chief officer rank. Your immediate predecessor was a slothful individual who did very little, and in your opinion allowed himself to be much too influenced by local politics and culture, so that he failed to assert the operational independence of the police from the government of the day.

There is known to be corruption in government circles to do with arms contracts, and you need inside information as to what is really going on and how many people are involved, before overt police action can be taken.

A source of considerable potential value is refusing to work for the police, despite their best efforts. You know Professor A to be three things:

- [ ] a distinguished scientist of international reputation;
- [ ] a long-term defence adviser to the ruling party; and
- [ ] a closet homosexual.

He is extremely discreet about his sexual orientation, which would be of great embarrassment to him if revealed publicly. Homosexuality is not a crime, but the nationalist party stands for traditional family values, and known homosexuals soon leave public life.

What is to be done?

Analysis

Before you decide what to do in this case, you may wish to decide the moral basis for your action in general. The simplest solution in this case is to import and impose a British moral/legal code, which would restrict your options. Whatever the possible gain, you would have no right, from the official British view, to blackmail your potential source, either personally or vicariously. Such methods are wrong and must be forbidden.

On the other hand, you are operating in a different country and context, where there may be a different view about the relationship between ends and means. Moreover, you are under pressure. After all, you have a duty to investigate a corruption scandal which may be of major public importance, and this could be your only way in. Does that mean different standards apply?

This is an opportunity for you to reinvent yourself as a moral person and exemplar, and decide what standards you would really wish to apply, and how to apply them.

....

COUNSELLING?

Inspector Da Silva wants advice, and has come to you although you are not his commander. In essence he tells you that he is suffering from severe stress and does not know what to do about it. He is sleeping badly, drinking too much, running up debts, and finding it difficult to make decisions at work that he should find relatively easy.

Da Silva is an ageing officer whose career has reached a plateau. He is now near retirement. He has a generally excellent record, with one or two minor blemishes. His family circumstances are difficult as his wife, who is much younger than he, is conspicuously and notoriously unfaithful to him. They have no children.

- ☐ How would you assess this situation?
- ☐ What else would you want to know?
- ☐ What are the options open to you?
- ☐ What would you do?

Analysis

Counselling raises many moral issues to do with confidentiality and trust, and if you are unfamiliar with established wisdom in this area it would be worth researching what has been learned. I would suggest that if literature does not give you the answers you need, that you speak to an established counsellor whom you know and trust as a person of experience and good judgement.

Meanwhile, there is a major issue about responsibility here, which in your anxiety to do good you may have overlooked: Inspector Da Silva has come to you *although you are not his commander.*

So, why has he come to you? Are you the right person to handle this? Do you have the counselling skills which could justify your involvement? What else might be required? Are you going to clear things first with Da Silva's official commander, before you take any action? If so, when does confidentiality begin? Having resolved all of that, what approach would you take? Does this case call for advice, referral or counselling? Whose interests should you serve? What are the competing priorities?

In this case we have given you more questions than answers. A little knowledge can be a dangerous thing, and counselling may be an area for you to think about further, rather than simply decide that you need to bolt on another 'skill', or find someone else who has it.

DECEPTION

A hard-working and conscientious police officer is rejected for a position in Special Branch on which she had set her heart, because she has close relatives who are politically unreliable. There is no suggestion that they have ever influenced Sgt Mildred Wagimbi, who is an exemplary police officer. Sgt Wagimbi asks if it were you who made the confidential enquiry into her background, and what you recommended. She has heard that it was you. It was, and you had suggested that she was unsuitable.

☐ What is going through your mind?
☐ What are your options?
☐ What will you say to her?

Analysis

As in all moral discussions, it is important to find and challenge the factual assumptions underlying policy. In this case, there is an assumption that because a trusted person has untrustworthy relatives, she cannot really be trusted – presumably because she may be liable to face undue pressure. Another way of putting this is in terms of risk: 'There is a risk of insecurity here, which a security-conscious organization cannot accept. No one actually distrusts you, Sergeant. But you do see the position, don't you?'

It would be better to start at the beginning, and create an algorithm for selection. The work may be secret: but the algorithm should be open.

— What is it that Sergeant Wagimbi (or another candidate) would like to do?
— Is there a vacancy?
— Is she suited to the work?
— Would her selection pose an undue security risk, and if so, why and how?
— If there is a problem, is there a way round it other than by rejecting this candidate?
— If you have to reject her (or any other candidate), how will you do so while at the same time applying the official values of the organization?

Most ethical codes refer to dealing with people with dignity. How are
you going to do that, in this case?

The big words here are honesty, confidentiality, dignity and fairness.

. . . .

DISTRESS

A young police sergeant has been showing signs of stress and her behaviour has become increasingly erratic and unreliable. As her manager you have been concerned about this, and have made efforts to find out whether or not there were any problems underlying her decline in performance.

Unfortunately, you have not been able to delve to the bottom of the matter. Sergeant Forrester is a quiet and reserved young woman who has never had much to say for herself, and until the past few months had carried out her duties in an unfussy and competent manner, suggesting that she was capable of more than was being asked. Consequently, her decline in performance, for which there is no obvious cause, is a mystery to you.

An interview leads nowhere. Sergeant Forrester fends off all your questions and offers of help, and insists that there are no problems. If there is anything wrong with her work, tell her what it is and she will correct it.

She is happy in the police service and finds the work both absorbing and fulfilling

☐   What are you going to do?

Analysis

The issue here is one of managerial obligations, responsibilities and limits. Skills are also involved, since someone else might have achieved something from the interview, which you did not.

— What is it reasonable for you to do? Where are the limits? Is your approach influenced by benevolent paternalism, because this is a woman in distress?
— If so, is that wrong?
— What will be the outcome for you if you do nothing, and Sergeant Forrester goes off the rails?
— What will be the outcome for the organization?
— What will be the outcome for her?

. . . .

DRESSAGE

1. You are working as a police area commander in a remote, rural and dangerous part of the United Kingdom, on exchange to the force there. You discover by accident that one of your most experienced (male) detectives is a transvestite who enjoys dressing up in women's clothing. He does not do so on duty, and you would have no idea of his proclivity but for a coincidental chain of events, whereby one of his colleagues saw and recognized him dressed as a woman in a bar in the regional centre. This ties in with other evidence, and there is no reasonable doubt that Chief Inspector MacMenamin is a transvestite.

Your immediate reaction is that this is no concern of yours. The officer's conduct is discreet, and he has not brought his force into disrepute. His conduct does not affect his work, and in today's climate of sexual tolerance it seems best ignored. There might be an issue about vulnerability, which you will need to think through, but it is not an immediate concern.

However, it soon becomes obvious that the officer who saw MacMenamin off duty has spread the story around, and there is a consensus of opinion that the transvestite will obviously be dismissed. You realize that in social terms this area is still an extremely conservative part of the world, and that you are facing the attitudes that might have been generally expressed in England 40 or 50 years ago. If you do nothing, you are likely to face censure or at least incomprehension, not only from the officers you command, but from your superiors within the police hierarchy.

☐   What will you do?

Variations

The following variations may or may not affect your reaction. Please consider why your policy might be different, and its ethical implications. I suggest that this exercise would be of more value carried out as a comparison of ideas with colleagues. Each variation is from the first example, and they are not cumulative.

2. MacMenamin realizes that his secret is out, and although no formal action has been taken he effectively suspends himself from duty, putting forward a variety of plausible reasons for non-attendance which you recognize to be excuses for avoiding his colleagues.

3. MacMenamin is at home on self-imposed absence. His wife, whom you barely know, comes in to see you. She is desperately worried about her husband, who appears extremely depressed and to be avoiding going to work. However, he has told her that everything is fine. His behaviour is most unlike him, and she cannot understand it. Is he under threat from a murderous terrorist organization, and trying not to worry her? Such cases are not unknown.

4. MacMenamin goes sick. There are procedures which you are supposed to follow, but they do not give you moral guidance as to how to treat this case.

5. MacMenamin asks for early retirement, claiming that his work has caused him to suffer stress. He has 25 years' service. If he can obtain retirement on medical grounds, he will have an excellent pension for life. If he simply retires, he will face a much less advantageous financial position. You have no previous evidence that he is suffering from stress, and his annual appraisals suggest that he is a balanced and robust individual. There is a procedure for dealing with such requests in your force, but it leaves a great deal open to interpretation, and offers no moral guidance. It is widely believed that at least some of the force's early retirements on medical grounds are unjustified by those criteria, and that managers are avoiding their responsibility to probe such claims.

6. MacMenamin is one of the few Roman Catholic officers in your area, and a good manager to boot. You are under pressure to recruit and retain Roman Catholic officers, other things being equal.

7. Before you have taken any action in MacMenamin's case, he dies in a car crash. The initial report indicates that he was driving alone, in good conditions, and on an undangerous road. There is no apparent reason why he lost control of the car and drove into a tree. He was sober. His funeral, which would normally be handled by the police unless the widow objected, needs to be arranged.

8. The officer in question is a woman, who enjoys dressing as a man.

9. The officer in question is a woman and closet lesbian.

10. The officer in question is a woman and declared lesbian.

Analysis

These scenarios raise a host of issues. An underlying theme is that of cultural and moral relativism. Cross-dressing is seen as profoundly wrong by one community, but not by another. What should you do when you cannot assume that others share your values? Challenge? Go with your conscience, and hope that others will understand your decision? Accept the majority view? How you proceed in this case will affect your whole relationship with the people you command, and the consequences of your decision must be considered. Other issues arising concern confidentiality, the morality of following standard procedures, welfare matters, fairness, and comparability.

Although the variations are based on the rather exotic case of Chief Inspector MacMenamin, the issues raised are universal. Your solutions to them all, I would suggest, must be able to stand up to scrutiny by the normal moral criteria as explored elsewhere in this book. The expedient solution – for example, in case 7, to treat the road crash as simply an event in isolation – may be justified; but the issues need to be thought through beforehand before it can be adopted.

ENCORE! ENCORE!

You have been asked to make a speech to a graduating class of police constables at the training school, which is commanded by an old friend of yours. He has suggested you include something about ethics. You decide to take him at his word and put across something serious on the subject.

Yours is a relatively clean force which attempts to reach a high standard of policing. However, public opinion believes the police to be corrupt, and there is some evidence to back this up in particular cases. Moreover, there is the question of national culture. Nepotism has been a fact of life in your community. Openly corrupt governmental officials have not always been charged or dismissed. The police, like other public servants, are relatively poorly paid; some citizens expect them to accept bribes or otherwise interpret their duties in a corrupt way, and are not outraged by this: it is a part of life.

☐   What are you going to say to the recruits, on the subject of ethics?
☐   To what standards will you refer?
☐   What support can they expect?
☐   What can you share with them?
☐   How will you put your message across?

Analysis

This is an opportunity to put theory into practice; or at least, to stand up for what you believe in.

....

FRIENDSHIP

You are old friends with another officer, Inspector Fadl'Allah, a highly effective CID commander, who has no time for modern police management jargon, but simply gets on with his job as he has always done it.

One evening, as you leave the station in the darkening gloom, you see him escorting a prisoner from a police car. You recognize the prisoner as Mohammed Farrukh, a well-known and brutal criminal, long suspected of armed robbery and murder, whom most members of the police service would have been wished to be hanged long ago.

You pass without comment, keen to go home and watch your favourite television programme. As you open your car you hear a sound which might have been a blow. Your mind is elsewhere and you pay it no real attention.

The next morning you notice when passing him in the corridor that Farrukh is severely marked about the face. He glares at you without speaking. Inspector Fadl'Allah, who is unmarked, gives you a broad smile.

☐ What are the underlying issues here?
☐ What action, if any, would you take?
☐ How far would you go?

Analysis

Clearly, you cannot ignore your suspicions. There is circumstantial evidence of police ill-treatment of a prisoner, and it would be fair to no one to do nothing. Strictly speaking, then, this is not a classic moral dilemma, in that you do not face two competing alternatives. Your overall duty is clear: to investigate further. It is how you go about making that investigation which is of interest. This case is included as a study in procedure and to illustrate the importance of routine. Police records will or should tell you, for example, what has happened to the person in question while he is in custody. Has he been injured? What were the circumstances? What if there is no record of injury? And how are you going to confront your friend?

GAY PRIDE

Your force has decided upon a campaign of positive action in recruiting suitable homosexual men and women to the service, with the intention of better representing the community which needs to be policed. What morally based arguments could you put forward to support this campaign against members of the public who regard it with disfavour?

Comment

It will require some skill to draft a set of arguments which convince, rather than simply expound a fashionable dogma. If we go back to Karl Popper, whom we left stranded: it is worth considering the very best case *against* your position that you can muster – and then answering it.

....

GYPSIES

You are working as a detective aide and are keen for your talents and enthusiasm to be recognized. As one of your first independent tasks you are given a spate of minor rural crimes to investigate. Preliminary inquiries draw a blank, whereupon a long-term member of CID advises you to find out if any gypsies have been seen in the area. Further conversation elicits that she has no particular reason to suggest that you look for gypsies, other than her long-held view that they are all thieves and that if there is a rural problem they are likely to be behind it.

You decide that your colleague has certainly allowed her views to become stereotyped, and possibly bigoted; and you determine to continue investigating the crimes with an open mind.

As it happens, you trace the crimes to a group of gypsies. Stolen property is found at their site, they are convicted, and you are commended. And your colleague? She is able to utter the immortal words: 'You see? What did I tell you? They're all thieves.'

☐   Is there an issue here?

Analysis

I think so, and this is an opportunity to apply some logic. However, not everyone warms to a preacher, and you need to consider how you would put your case.

HEROINE

A prisoner under interrogation claims that she has important information to offer you, which will help you solve a number of serious crimes. Janet MacLeod is an American traveller and heroin addict, desperate for her next fix. She says that she will say nothing more unless she is given heroin. You believe her.

This is a problem. The chief constable has told you to solve more crimes, and there is a reasonable expectation that giving the junkie what she wants will help you to do so. However, the use of heroin is illegal in your country, and the drug cannot be obtained from a doctor. On the other hand, you also know that the drugs squad has recently seized a large amount of 'pure' heroin, which will not be needed as evidence.

☐ What are the issues here?
☐ What will you do?

Analysis

From an absolute point of view, your duty is clear – or appears so. It is not the role of the police service to resolve the public's medical problems, and it is certainly not your role to break the law yourself. Whatever might be gained from helping Janet MacLeod, you cannot do so.

On the other hand, from the utilitarian point of view, the balance of happiness would be served by your breaking the law. Janet MacLeod will be happier, and you will have your information – which may mean that fewer people suffer harm in the future.

Consequentially, it is hard to assess the better course of action. If you supply Janet Macleod with heroin and it becomes known that you have done so, then you will either be prosecuted, or your organization will be operating with dual standards.

. . . .

LECTURE

You are a senior police officer who has been asked to lecture on police ethics at the national police academy, of which you are a graduate and which you have long supported. In theory, this is a great honour. In practice, lectures at the academy tend to have little visible impact, and you have often wondered if the effort is worthwhile. Nevertheless, you agreed to give the talk, and in collaboration with your staff officer have spent some time in preparing for it.

Your talk is programmed for the Wednesday of the fourth and final week of an operational commanders' programme at the academy. On the Monday, you realize that although it is not impossible, it will be extremely difficult for you to meet this commitment. NB There are no legal implications in this scenario. You could not be sued for breach of contract. This is a gentleman's understanding, not a service level agreement. Here is a summary of the options open to you:

1. To put your operational commitment first, and say nothing to the academy. They are training senior police officers, after all. Such officers know the realities of police work, and the pressures on senior officers' time. If the lecturer does not appear, they will find something else to do.
2. To apologize and withdraw as soon as possible.
3. To apologize, indicate the difficulties which have arisen, and attempt to resolve the problem by negotiating an alternative time, providing a text of what you were going to say, suggesting an alternative (and available) speaker of equivalent value, or in some other way positively addressing the dilemma by attempting to meet both your needs and those of the academy.
4. To keep your commitment to the academy with no further ado.

☐   Which option would you choose, and why?

Discussion

Although this might appear a relatively trivial dilemma, it lays bare one of the fundamental ethical issues: keeping one's word. The fourth option is the clearest, and one which some moral philosophers would defend strongly. One should never break a commitment under any circumstances. In other words, having agreed to give this lecture, you should give it unless it be physically impossible. The potential value of the lecture, the possibility of its substitution, and the importance of other claims upon your time are tempting but irrelevant factors. Keep your word, because it is the right thing to do.

The problem with this position is that it is inflexible. If good decisions are based upon a rational analysis of competing alternatives, then simply to keep your word under any circumstances may not be the right thing to do. Certainly, you should not break a commitment simply because to keep it might be awkward or inconvenient for you. But here, it may well be that there are more important claims upon your time than to give the lecture. In this situation you need to ask yourself:

- [ ] What are the pros and cons of the various options?
- [ ] Who gains, and who loses?
- [ ] What are your real motives?

Introspection – looking within oneself, and mulling over what one finds – was a method recommended and practised by nineteenth century psychologists. It fell out of fashion as some psychologists moved towards experimentation as a method of understanding behaviour, and Freud and his followers postulated the existence of subconscious or even unconscious motives for our behaviour. If some thing is subconscious, then introspection cannot reveal it.

Our position is neither behaviourist nor Freudian, but pragmatic. Experience shows that introspection can be a useful activity. Calm and objective reflection will often tell us our true motives.

Two other useful questions are these:

- [ ] Which decision can you defend most robustly, and over the longest period?
- [ ] Can you use lateral thinking to do the impossible, and satisfy both commitments?

PERSUASION

You have been appointed chief of police in a sleepy little town, miles from the capital. Your predecessor as chief served for 30 years under the previous regime, on the basis of whom rather than what he knew. While not especially corrupt, he was a political animal with little or no interest in establishing a professional and effective police service for the people of the area. Rather, he saw his role as to keep the regime (and himself) in power, and he was prepared to bend the rules to do so – often with the tacit or explicit approval of the local party bosses. As an example of his partial behaviour, when the local mayor's son killed a gypsy in a drunken brawl, the chief of police was able to smooth things over so that no official action was taken. The son's conduct might have been justified as self-defence, but that was never decided by a court.

The reputation of the police in Slivograd is not high, and nor is the self-esteem and morale of the officers whom you are about to command. Both district and police are used to a slow, inefficient, and arbitrary system of policing, wherein the police have made and enforced the rules as they chose.

You are a professional and dedicated police officer who is determined to turn things around, and to introduce proper policing to the district.

Outline your strategy for doing so.

☐ How will you deal with your policemen and women, who do
    not necessarily share your aims – at least at the moment?
☐ How will you convince the local people, that change is here to stay?

Commentary

This problem allows for the utilization of experience, which experienced police officers should enjoy.

PRESSURE

You are the senior CID officer for a police area, whose major headache is a circle of suspected criminals against whom you have so far made no headway. You suspect that they are involved in all sorts of crimes, including drugs, fraud, theft and handling stolen goods: but so far you have not been able to come up with anything concrete against them. You have to recognize that they are very well organized and extremely security-conscious: so much so, in fact, that you have sometimes wondered if they have had training or advice from an organization such as the IRA, or a bent copper or employee of the security service. The gang has proved impervious to police penetration.

One evening a traffic officer arrests Jesse Rosen for drunken driving. Rosen is very drunk and will certainly lose his licence and probably go to prison if the case is pursued. If that happens, he must lose his job as a travelling salesman, and lose the position in society by which he apparently sets much store.

It just so happens that his elder brother Micah is the prime suspect to be the ring-leader of the gang you wish to penetrate. You have had no reason to suspect Jesse of criminal involvement.

☐ What would you do next?

NB: we wish to explore applied ethics, and not compare knowledge of regulations. Please assume that for the purposes of the exercise, your force has no rules or regulations in place as to how informants should be recruited or used, and that any decisions which you make need only be based upon your common sense and good judgement, together with your interpretation of such laws as may apply.

PROSTITUTION

The situation

You are the new commander in an inner-city area where there is an emerging problem to do with prostitution and kerb-crawling. Traditionally, prostitution has been tolerated in the area. The vice squad has taken a spasmodic interest, and prostitutes have been occasionally fined for street offences. Otherwise, there has been little or no action.

Developments

However, times have changed. More and more men are coming to the district by car, and driving around looking for prostitutes. Some of the women whom they accost are not prostitutes and are highly offended; and there is a ground-swell of local opinion that the police must do something to address this issue.

Local concern

You attend a local community meeting, where you are told that it is not enough to keep the problem 'under review'. The community wants a radical shift in the police attitude and policy in regard to a serious social problem.

The initial reaction

Your officers are fatalistic. As they indicate:

— prostitution is an age-old problem, which no one will eradicate;
— legal remedies are limited, and the new law on kerb-crawling is difficult to enforce;
— displacing or suspending the problem is not the same as resolving it;
— police resources could be better used elsewhere;
— prostitutes provide useful information.

Action can of course be taken, but it will be more placatory than a real solution.

What will you do?

Comment

Clearly, prostitution is an old problem; but not necessarily quite so intractable as is here assumed. Although there is common sense in what your officers say, their attitude is pessimistic rather than positive, and some of their assumptions could be challenged. Considering this dilemma is a way into exploring the reality of the notion of policing by consent.

A useful reference: *Kerb-crawling, Prostitution and Multi-Agency Policing*, Roger Matthews, Home Office Crime Prevention Unit Paper 43, London 1993.

THEFT WITH MENACES

A gang of criminals take a motor car to carry out an armed robbery, telling the owner it will be returned to him in 24 hours. Meanwhile, he is to say nothing. (If he reports the theft, the usual practice is that the car will be put on the Police National Computer as stolen. It is then likely to be stopped by any police patrol. If not, there is no record that it is stolen and the gang is not likely to be stopped on the way to the robbery.)

The owner, a public-spirited citizen, informs the police of the whole circumstances as soon as the theft has occurred, and before the armed robbery can have taken place. At the same time, Mr Soulis says that he is convinced that the gang are ruthless, died-in-the-wool criminals, and he is worried about the safety of his wife and family.

You are the police commander for the area, and need to decide what to do.

Analysis

This is a dilemma about priorities and risks. Mr Soulis has in effect become a police informant, and you need to protect him and his family, while at the same time making sure that his information is not wasted. You now face a practical problem: how can you catch the robbers without their realizing that Mr Soulis betrayed them?

The application of standard informant-handling policy should help here, and this problem be resolved without undue difficulty.

TRUST

While visiting a well-known and very expensive restaurant – not the sort of place you normally frequent – you notice a police colleague, Supt Arnolfini, deep in conversation with a known criminal who is often referred to as a Mr Big, and who is rumoured to have a coterie of government and police officials on his payroll.

Supt Arnolfini is a senior police officer, well liked and respected in the force for his ability to get things done. He has worked both in special branch and CID in the past and he is now working at headquarters. You are not quite sure of his official duties, as his job title is written in management jargon and means nothing.

Supt Arnolfini is married, has several children, and leads an expansive life style, often holidaying abroad or on his yacht. He is open about living beyond his police salary and has often extolled the merits of marrying for money: his wife comes from a rich family who have considerable business interests in your community. You have had no reason to be suspicious of your colleague in the past.

☐ What would you do?

Analysis

In this case you have a clear duty to act, and the only purpose of the dilemma is to encourage reflection on precisely why and how this should be done. You have, after all, only two real options: to do nothing, and to act upon your suspicions.

To do nothing contradicts so many principles that we need not list them all. First, it would be unfair. You are leaving someone under suspicion, even if it be only circumstantial, rather than giving him the opportunity to clear his name. If, as it happens, Arnolfini *is* up to no good, then this needs to be known. His privacy, status and reputation, and the accidental means by which suspicion emerged, are surely of lesser importance than that an investigation appears necessary.

Secondly, you are a police officer, and must put the interests of the organization, and the public, before the possible interests of Supt Arnolfini. (As we have established, this clash is more apparent than real. It is in the Superintendent's interests that his name be cleared.)

How to do it? In this case, you will need to act cautiously and with discretion. Your actions should not be unreasonable. Whose reasoning should we use? The hypothetical observer? Certainly. Or how about the Superintendent himself?

Imagine that you are having to explain what you did and why to the man in question, the case being over. What would you say? How would you defend what you chose to do?

UNDERGROUND

Under your command is a long-service officer who has proved particularly useful at undercover work, in which he has effectively specialized since he joined CID about ten years ago. Detective Constable Redgrave has been commended by more than one chief constable and judge for his efforts, which have lead to many arrests. On one occasion he spent more than six months penetrating a drugs gang in highly difficult and dangerous circumstances. In order to live his cover he became a drug-user himself, but was since able to free himself of the habit.

Mark Redgrave appears a contented and balanced individual who has been able to cope with the long-term pressures of undercover work. His work has become an addiction to him, but it is an addiction with which he and his wife appear contented: Mrs Redgrave has a business in her own right, and the Redgraves have no children. Her husband's sometimes prolonged absences and need to maintain a dual identity are not an apparent problem.

That situation should no longer continue. Force policy says that no-one should remain in CID indefinitely, and Redgrave has been in longer than most. You should return him to uniform and give someone else the chance to work in CID. If you do so, you anticipate that this officer will simply leave the police service and take his talents elsewhere. You are on the horns of a dilemma. Do you follow the spirit of force policy, or spin things out and keep Redgrave where he is?

Commentary

This is a conflict of duty in which the interests of the officer, his manager and the organization do not necessarily coincide. You will wish to be fair: but fair to whom? The officer who has given good service to CID already, or the officers who have not yet had the opportunity to show what they can do?

In absolutist terms, policy is policy, and you have a duty to enact it and to serve the wider interests of the organization.

Consequentially, to follow this policy in this case will mean that CID is temporarily disadvantaged, since this officer's skills cannot, presumably, be immediately replaced. Pragmatically speaking, something might be arranged. For example, could Mark Redgrave be persuaded to pass on some of his experience and expertise to the organization, even if he were to stop working undercover? Is he really as opposed to uniform work as you suppose?

ZEAL

You oversee the work of a number of police officers in a busy inner city area, where there is a good deal of miscellaneous violence. Many police officers have been attacked and it has become customary, although not invariable, for them to patrol the town centre in pairs, especially late at night. Patrolling officers are armed with the new extending (metal) baton, which can be used as a weapon of offence. Despite this new acquisition, morale is still low.

You realize when scanning records that one of your officers, Michael Johnson, has attracted a large number of complaints – more than any other officer. Constable Johnson is a small man with a very strong physique. He used to be a member of the Special Boat Service, and still trains fanatically in the gymnasium every day. Constable Johnson is a popular and respected member of his shift, who plays a full part in its sporting and social activities. He has put a tremendous effort into raising money for handicapped children, for which he is known throughout the force and has received national publicity. Constable Johnson is perfectly happy to patrol the town centre alone, and often does so. He has a good arrest record and is well-known to local people. Most of the complaints against him relate to the excessive use of force in making arrests. No prisoner has been seriously injured and no complaint has received more than an informal investigation.

Constable Johnson comes across as a man with a calm and restrained personality, very set in his views. He knows what is right and what is wrong, and once he has made his mind up is very unlikely to change it. He enjoys his work as a constable and has no ambitions for promotion. He is aged 38 and has served eight years in the police. He is a married man with no children, and is a gifted water-colourist.

☐   What are the options open to you here?
☐   What action would you take in this case?

Commentary

As usual, the same activity can be viewed in different ways. Constable Johnson is a competent, respected and effective police officer who performs his duties zealously. Circumstantial evidence suggests that he may be over-zealous, and would be a better officer if his behaviour could be adjusted slightly. However, circumstantial evidence can be misleading, and it may be that this interpretation is wrong. In any case, it could be bitterly resented. How would you approach this issue? How do you think he would react to your approach? How could you reach common ground?

APPENDIX

The Warrnambool method

This is a logical and systematic approach to ethical problem solving which enables a group to focus its energy towards resolving a problem presented by one of its members. It is a useful framework for anyone to use who is unfamiliar with formal ethical analysis.

1. What is the problem?

☐ Recognition that an ethical problem exists, and that it is right and proper to address it.
☐ The involvement of the person who is relating the problem.
☐ The problem, in outline.
☐ Previously attempted solutions, if applicable, with reasons for their failure.
☐ Most ethical problems can be described in terms of a choice between two alternatives, each of which has disadvantages. What are they, in this case?

2. What is your aim?

Your aim should be positive, clear, in accord with your responsibilities, and the utmost you can do under the circumstances. It does not include your plan of action.

3. What are the possible options?

☐ Go beyond what was already discussed under *1*. Brainstorm. Suspend disbelief. Suspend moral judgement.

4. Analysis

a. First, simply list the advantages and disadvantages of each option, according to whatever criteria the group uses.
   b. Secondly, work through the list and cluster the factors, as they have emerged. Here are some possibilities:

☐ Political constraints.
☐ Legal considerations.
☐ Financial and resource implications.

- ☐ Technical aspects.
- ☐ Environmental factors.
- ☐ Ethical status.
- ☐ Consequences.

Risk
1. Probability of failure.
2. Severity of consequences.

Which factors seem most important? Is there one single overriding factor?

Can you impose an ethical template on the discussion? For example, is some sort of utilitarian calculation possible? Is there an absolute moral factor?

    c. Ask everyone to state their conviction.

    d. Allow the consensus to emerge.

5. Choose, plan and apply the solution

6. Monitor and evaluate the outcome

The role of the Devil's Advocate

It is suggested that the group should have a Devil's Advocate, as well as a chairman. The DA should be:

- ☐ trusted by the group;
- ☐ intelligent but not opinionated;
- ☐ disinterested in the solution achieved;
- ☐ not in a position of overwhelming authority;
- ☐ ethically aware but not pedantic;
- ☐ concise, logical and assertive.

It makes sense to separate the roles of chairman and DA, and ensure their skills and personalities mesh productively. You do not want two shapers!

8
POLICING PROTEST AND DISSENT

. . . .

ACTIVITY

You are the police officer in charge of a part of the country where there is a deep division between Zoroastrians and animists, to the extent that in reality you have to police two communities. For historical reasons, very few animists trust the police, which is a predominantly Zoroastrian force. (Animists represent about 25 per cent of the population in this part of the country, and Zoroastrians about 60 per cent. The remainder do not align with either camp.)

Summer has arrived, and with it the marching season. Every year the Zoroastrians celebrate their collective identity by marching along historically-defined routes, led by Zoroastrian priests dressed in white and bearing burning orbs. Once upon a time this caused little difficulty, and was even accepted as an absorbing spectacle: but over the course of the years, changes of population have taken place, and what was once Zoroastrian territory is now in many cases animist. The politicized animists object to the marches, which they see as an expression of Zoroastrian triumphalism: and objection has led to protest, demonstration, disorder and rioting. The Zoroastrians have announced that they intend to march to the centre of your local town next Saturday morning, as they have always done: and the animists have said that they will protest the march. Significantly, a leading animist has indicated that he cannot guarantee to control the behaviour of his followers; and in your opinion there is likely to be disorder.

....

Task

Your task is to devise a policy which will be both fair and effective in keeping the peace.

Commentary

This is clearly a difficult task, and under some circumstances it could amount to an impossible one. The senior police officer needs to attempt to reconcile competing priorities and hope that they do not prove to be irreconcilable.

Upholding the rule of law

The senior officer has a duty to uphold the rule of law. If he has the authority to ban a march for good and sufficient reasons, and if those reasons apply on this occasion, then he should ban it. This policy would have the advantage that he would be seen to be acting impartially, ie in the interests of the wider community, and not just one section of it (which happens to be heavily represented in his police force).

This policy sounds fair: but can he make the ban effective? The senior officer needs to consider what resources he may need if he is to attempt to police the majority, and what consequences may follow from their use.

Keeping the peace

Upholding the rule of law and keeping the peace may or may not go together. In this case, the senior officer needs to weigh up the likely consequences of his actions and shape his plans accordingly. If banning the march is likely to cause greater disruption than allowing it to happen, then there is a case for allowing the march to proceed – even if this is likely to be interpreted as the police favouring the Zoroastrians at the expense of the animists.

Building community relationships

The problem is to devise a fair and effective policy for keeping the peace next Saturday. However, any sensible police officer will consider the longer-term implications of his actions, as well as the immediate problem he needs to solve. Whichever policy he chooses, what are its

. . . .

likely long-term consequences for community relationships? Policing by consent, in which the force believes, means building and maintaining strong relationships with the local community. Yes; but which community? The two religious communities have conflicting aims, and compromise may not be possible. If the plan be to allow the march to proceed under strict police supervision, then how will the force restore its relationship with the animist section of the population, who will have seen their wishes ignored?

Policing in a political context

Under the British system of policing, operational decisions are entirely the decision of the chief constable. He is responsible for deciding what happens on Saturday: and provided that his proposed actions are lawful, he need consult no one. The police authority has no say in operational matters. Nor does the mayor, the local MP, or anyone else in parliament, including the Home Secretary.

However, these and others are all interested parties, and a wise senior officer will have reflected upon their views. Should the police policy contradict local, regional or national political objectives, or should the police operation go disastrously wrong, then the senior officer is liable to be criticized by many people, some of whom may reflect on his ability to understand and acknowledge political objectives. It is not unethical to consider the political context in which decisions are made.

. . . .

The activity over which you have just pondered raises in an acute form the difficulties of policing a divided community. In such a situation it may only be possible to police by authority, and the police may not be able to be both fair to all and keep the peace. Great Britain is not a divided community as imagined in our example, and our political traditions tend to emphasize compromise and consensus rather than confrontation – or so we should like to believe. The prevailing political philosophy in this country is that of liberal democracy. We need to explore what this means, and to consider its implications for policing.

ON LIBERTY

John Stuart Mill (1806–1873) is the father of modern liberalism, with its emphasis upon the freedom of the individual to make moral (and other) choices. What are the underlying assumptions upon which his thought rested, and upon which the notion of a liberal democracy has been created?

1. People are fundamentally both rational and good. The two go together.
2. Civilized people share certain values. Government will not need to exercise draconian powers to control anti-social behaviour, because such behaviour is fundamentally irrational.
3. Government is necessary, and may use force on occasion, because people will not always be either rational or good; but the power of government must be circumscribed to prevent tyranny.

Mill's fundamental principle

Mill believed in democracy, at least for civilized communities; but he sought to avoid the tyranny of the majority. If democracy simply means rule by the majority, then he feared its potential for evil. After all, the majority might be ignorant of, indifferent towards, or even vindictive about the well-being of a minority within its midst.

Such minorities need not be taken to consist only of obviously disadvantaged groups, who may be actively discriminated against on grounds of race, sex or disability. Anyone whose tastes, opinions or habits are not in tune with the majority, on any issue, may be subjected to the tyranny of the majority – unless there are safeguards.

'You want to smoke *tobacco*? Well, you can't!'

Democracy, in its original Greek sense, was direct. It meant rule by the people. How did it work? You gathered together all male, free, local citizens and they decided issues there and then. (Slaves, foreigners, women and children were excluded from the process.) Officials were elected by the people to carry out its wishes for a strictly limited period, and were then held to personal account for what they had done. This meant, presumably, that you could turn up on the appropriate hillside to say your piece on the price of bread, and find yourself in command of the Athenian Navy.

This immensely appealing system (for Athenian freemen) could lead to demagoguery and mob rule, as anti-democratic writers such as Plato recognized; and in the modern world it has been largely replaced by representative democracy. However, even within a representative system a majority can trample on the minority. There are various ways by which you can design to safeguard the rights of minority groups by weakening the absolute power of the simple majority. You may do so by complicating the system, or by building in safeguards; or both. For example:

☐ You may produce a written constitution, formally limiting the powers of government. The constitution may guarantee certain rights to the ordinary citizen.

☐ You may appoint a supreme court to guard against infringements of the constitution, and amend it as the notion of rights develops.

☐ You may create a parliamentary system of more than one chamber, or adopt proportional representation, or both, so that no one group can exert a tyrannical influence.

☐ You may formally separate legislative, judiciary and executive, so that the laws are made, interpreted and enforced by different bodies.

☐ You may duplicate parts of your executive, as for example in France, where the *police nationale* and the *gendarmerie* share responsibility for policing and report to different ministries.

☐ You may make the police responsible to two sets of masters, as in The Netherlands, where police forces are accountable to both local and regional political representatives at the same time.

☐ There are a host of other ways in which you can weaken or dilute the power of the simple majority to dictate the life of the ordinary citizen, by building in checks and balances throughout the system. Thus in Great Britain, we do not have a single, national police service, but a number of different forces with both local and national responsibilities, accountable to a range of organizations. Partly this is the result of historical accident, and the disinclination of the British to design a system from first principles. But it is also a recognition of the liberal principle that power should be divided.

Mill subscribed to general liberal notions about the limitation and separation of power. He set out his recommendation for avoiding the tyranny of the majority very clearly in his seminal essay, 'On Liberty', from which I quote:

> The object of this essay is to assert one very simple principle, as entitled to govern absolutely the dealings of society with the individual

in the way of compulsion and control, whether the means used be physical force in the form of legal penalties, or the moral coercion of public opinion. That principle is, that the sole end for which mankind are warranted, individually or collectively, in interfering with the liberty of action of any of their number, is self-protection. That the only purpose for which power may rightfully be exercised over any member of a civilised community, against his will, is to prevent harm to others. His own good, either physical or moral, is not a sufficient warrant. He cannot rightfully be compelled to do or forbear because it will be better for him to do so, because it will make him happier, because, in the opinion of others, to do so would be wise, or even right. These are good reasons for remonstrating with him, or reasoning with him, or persuading him, or entreating him, but not for compelling him, or visiting him with any evil in case he do otherwise. To justify that, the conduct from which it is desired to deter him, must be calculated to produce evil to someone else. The only part of the conduct of anyone, for which he is amenable to society, is that which concerns others. In the part which merely concerns himself, his independence is, of right, absolute. Over himself, over his own body and mind, the individual is sovereign.

Reflection

Mill's essay, 'On Liberty', has had an enormous impact upon both thinking and legislation in the years since it was first published in 1859. It is the creed of libertarianism. The real question is this: does it work? Can we divide acts into those which affect ourselves and those which affect other people? The great Victorian judge James Fitzjames Stephen thought not, and in his book, *Liberty, Fraternity, Equality*, he attacked Mill, 'the book in breeches', hook, line and sinker. Mill's principle was unworkable, he declared, because we cannot divide acts between those which affect only the perpetrator and those which affect others. Every action affects other people. Secondly, Fitzjames Stephen considered that the state has the right to promote good behaviour, and should not shrink from castigating behaviour which it considers morally wrong.

'I do not think the state ought to stand bandying compliments with pimps.'

In a prescient passage, Stephen parodies a disciple of John Stuart Mill attempting not to give offence in addressing a man of low morals:

Without offence to your better judgement, dear Sir, and without presuming to set up my opinion against yours, I beg to observe that I am entitled for certain purposes to treat the question whether your views are right as one which admits of two opinions. I am far from expressing absolute condemnation of an experiment in living from which I dissent ... [but] venture, with the greatest deference, to call upon you not to exercise your profession. (p. 137).

Having set up his opponent, Stephen then expresses his real opinion:

My feeling is that if society gets its grip on the collar of such a fellow it should say to him: 'You dirty rascal, it may be a question whether you should be suffered to remain in your native filth untouched, or whether my opinion about you should be printed by the lash on your bare back. That question will be settled without the slightest reference to your wishes or feelings; but as to the nature of my opinion about you, there can be no question at all.' Most people, I think, would feel that the latter form of address is at all events the more natural. (p. 138).

The debate between Mill and Stephen has been repeated a century later, between Professor H L A Hart (1963; 1968) and Lord Devlin (1963), the former taking and amplifying Mill's case, and the latter Stephen's. Both produce excellent arguments, which are worth reading in full and which I will not attempt to summarize here. There are two comments I shall make about Lord Devlin's contribution to the debate. First, Lord Devlin acknowledges that Great Britain is no longer a nation of practising Christians, and that therefore we cannot link religion, ethics and law as we might have done in the past. Nevertheless, he is interested in the relationship between morality and law, and believes that the state has a duty to enforce common morality. How is that morality to be discovered, in the absence of a universal religion? Devlin considers and rejects the notion of allowing it to be decided by intellectual prowess, and puts his faith in the jury as the voice of the people. If someone be accused, for example, of conspiring to corrupt public morals, then Devlin feels it is up to the ordinary people (for that is what a jury is) to determine whether or not public morality has been transgressed. This is an extremely interesting argument. It would nowadays put the determination of morality in the hands of the Crown Prosecution Service, since it is that organization which decides what goes before a jury.

Secondly, although Lord Devlin wrote only a generation ago, his ideas on what the public would or would not stand for have been overtaken by the revolution in sexual morality which has taken place in the past 30 years.

For example, until 1963 homosexuality was illegal and punishable by imprisonment. In 1957 the Wolfenden Committee, basing its arguments very much on Millian grounds, recommended that homosexuality should be allowed between consenting adults in private; and in 1963 the crusading Home Secretary Roy Jenkins was able to get a series of reformist measures through parliament. His reforms led to what was labelled the 'permissive society', although he called it a civilised one.

From 1963 to 1996 is only 33 years – barely more than the length of a police officer's service. What is the position of homosexuality now? As we all know, there has been a profound change. The law remains the same. Although there have been attempts to reduce the age of consent to the same as that for heterosexual sex, they have not succeeded. Legally tolerated homosexuality begins at 18. However, what used to be a discreet activity has come into the open. Once homosexuality, whether legal or illegal, was more or less tolerated so long as its adherents pursued their inclination in secret. Homosexuals and lesbians now openly parade their sexual orientation and partnerships, and want rights. (Some) homosexuals want marriage, the right to adopt children, and an end to any form of discrimination. Some oppose the continuing ban on the employment of homosexuals in the armed forces. As a special interest group they are engaging in dialogue with the police service, and in some areas they are joining the police service as declared homosexuals and lesbians.

Does that mean that there has been a wholesale revolution in public attitudes? Wherever you go in the United Kingdom, will you find that the great majority of people make no distinction between heterosexuality and homosexuality? Far from it: prejudice, discrimination and dislike are with us still, and the majority still believes homosexuality to be wrong. What there may have been, perhaps, is some acceptance of Mill's principle, that there are certain things which may be disapproved yet tolerated, in that the power of the state would be used inappropriately against them.

So, are we progressing towards Mill's ideal of tolerance and coexistence based upon reason? Not entirely. In a multi-racial and multi-cultural society, some of the people who now make up a significant proportion of the population of Great Britain have no tradition of liberal democracy in their past, and a distinct, logical and religiously-defensible set of beliefs, attitudes and prejudices of their own – which the police, as the impartial arbiters of acceptable behaviour, need to take into account. It is not my ambition to compare the religious, political and social beliefs of Islam with those which have evolved in Great Britain over a very long period. Such a comparison would require a book of its own, and the appropriate scholarship to write it. But it would be foolish to ignore this issue, and to leave intact the presumption that there has been no change in our society. Any police officer who works in a multi-racial area needs to think about the core values of those whom he polices, and how they can be fitted into his equation for successful policing.

Reform as a beginning and not an end

Reformers often rather naively believe that only one last adjustment needs to be made, in order for everything to be perfect. Thus, Lord Grey's intention in promoting the Great Reform Act of 1832 was to make a final adjustment to the franchise, by extending the right to vote in parliamentary elections to the 40-shilling freeholder (a minority of the adult male population). In fact, the Great Reform Act roused rather than satisfied expectations, and was the precursor of further reforms culminating in universal suffrage. It would seem likely, other things being equal, that the reforms in regard to sexual freedom begun in 1963 will eventually culminate in a legislative framework which allows total sexual freedom. We have already seen sado-masochists claiming that they should not be prosecuted for damaging each other, since the suffering is inflicted by consent; and there is an active group lobbying on behalf of sexual intercourse with children – which is usually prosecuted as child abuse. One does not have to be James Fitzjames Stephen to express one's views forcibly on that supposed freedom: but it is possible that even in the area of sexual intercourse between adults and children, what has traditionally been forbidden or discouraged will become permissible, if not approved.

ACTIVITY

You are the new police sergeant in a quiet, isolated and remote rural area. The local people are not very helpful to the police, and tend to avoid taxes, regulations, permits, licences and all the other paraphernalia of the modern and highly bureaucratic state. Unless you make yourself busy you do not have much to do, as little crime is brought to your attention. As you get to know the area and its inhabitants better, you hear the gossip: and the gossip is that incest is on the increase. At first, you are inclined to dismiss this as tittle-tattle, but then names are mentioned – brothers and sisters who live together and have never married, and other examples. You make some very discreet inquiries, but get nowhere. If anyone is practising incest, they are keeping it very quiet; and there is no evidence that an incestuous couple has produced children.

☐ Would you carry your investigations further, or let sleeping dogs lie?
☐ On what moral principles would your decision be based?

Commentary

No doubt any busy inner-city officer, reading this, will be saying to himself: I wish I had that sergeant's problems! It is a common police practice, and one that can easily be justified on ethical grounds, not to go looking for trouble. If there is a problem in a rural community, the police officer will hear about it sooner or later – and to hear sooner may require a disproportionate effort. On the other hand, it is the duty of the police officer to uphold the law, and the law forbids incest.

In this situation, the police officer must attempt to gauge the range and strength of public opinion. Is something going on? Are people concerned about it? What would be the consequences of being seen to do nothing? When are the poison-pen letters likely to start, if they are not already flowing? Who will be writing them? These are mainly practical questions, rather than specifically ethical ones; and the police officer is normally more concerned with a breach of the peace than a breach of morality. However, the two intermesh.

SELF-REGARDING AND OTHER-REGARDING ACTS: MILL'S PRINCIPLE APPLIED

The libertarian debate is with us still, and in the real world it is not always easy to apply Mill's 'very simple principle'. Here are five areas for further examination.

Violence

If someone is a bully, thug or rapist, then we can apply the principle very easily. The actions of the bully, thug or rapist are clearly intended to do harm to others, and the state is entitled to use both physical force and moral coercion in combating them.

Vandalism

What are we to do about the vandal? I refer to the youth who attacks what local authorities quaintly call 'street furniture', who damages cars, gardens and sheds, but leaves people alone. We could argue that he is not a member of a civilized community, but I do not think Mill would have worn that, since he distinguishes between communities as a whole, and not the people within them. There is barbarism and there are civilized societies; but there are not, in Mill's world, barbarians within civilized societies. Is the vandal's behaviour to be left uncorrected, because it affects only property? I think not. There is a gap in Mill's theory here. The state is entitled to use compulsion against vandals.

Tobacco

If we examine the issue of smoking tobacco, then what would appear at first sight a workable distinction between self-regarding acts and those which affect other people becomes problematic under closer scrutiny. The citizen who smokes tobacco is free to indulge in something which has been shown to be potentially injurious, because the consequences are injurious to himself rather than others. The state has attempted, to use Mill's verbs, to remonstrate, reason with, persuade and entreat the smoker to stop, to a very strong degree. Thus, for example:

- [ ] Every pack of cigarettes carries a government health warning, and is heavily taxed.
- [ ] The advertising of tobacco is severely restricted.
- [ ] Tobacconists are forbidden to sell their wares to children (a rule with which Mill would have certainly agreed, since he stated that liberty was only for mature members of civilized communities).
- [ ] A large, government-sponsored industry spends the taxpayer's money on advertising campaigns which point out the dangers of smoking.

☐ Smoking is banned altogether in many areas.

The government has stopped there. It has not compelled the smoker to put out his pipe. The Minister of Health is free to smoke, if he or she wishes, and so is any judge, civil servant or police officer. This would appear a successful practical application of Mill's principle, but its success is under pressure.

First, there is a lobby of people who claim that so-called passive smoking is injurious to the health of others. In other words, being near other peoples' tobacco smoke can harm you. Therefore, smoking is not a self-regarding act. Therefore, smoking should be made even more difficult, or banned altogether – and those who have suffered its ill effects through no fault of their own should be compensated.

Secondly, some doctors have challenged the notion that the liberty of the individual should be sacrosanct, because of the hidden costs of his misbehaviour for others – and any tax-payer is entitled to put the same argument. Let us suppose that someone chooses to smoke, despite clear, accessible and scientifically validated advice that it may be damaging his health. Let us go further, and suppose that someone chooses to continue to smoke, despite clear evidence that it *is* damaging his health. The smoker contracts lung cancer, and comes to the National Health Service for help. Should he be given every benefit which the service can offer? Even though he brought his misfortune upon himself, at least to some extent, and to treat him must mean that there is less opportunity to treat others? Clearly, there is a profound ethical dilemma here, which we would need to analyse further with the use of words like 'choice', 'responsibility' and 'fairness' if we wished to delve deeper. (It is also interesting to note that the British Medical Association offers advice on such dilemmas, just as we would like a police institute to do.)

For our present purposes, what is clear is that in a world of inter-dependency, Mill's very simple principle does not work. To paraphrase John Dunne, no act is an island. The distinction Mill makes, in which we can clearly and simply distinguish between acts which only affect ourselves and those which affect others, is a fantasy. It is a pleasant fantasy for a libertarian. It is a plausible fantasy, because it is possible to think of acts which appear *primarily* self-regarding. And it is a necessary fantasy, since Mill was right to put forward some principle to attempt to limit the power of the state, whether autocratically or democratically determined, to interfere in the life of the ordinary citizen; and his principle gives us a basis for constructive debate within an agreed framework.

Alcohol

Alcohol is a drug which can have appalling effects in terms of addiction, degradation and violence. Alcohol can destroy both people and societies. The British approach has been to tolerate the production, sale and consumption of alcohol, but to regulate all three activities very closely. This involves considerable work for the police, and it is noticeable that as one restriction is lifted, another is imposed. Thus, the licensing laws have been relaxed, so that public houses can stay open in the afternoon, if they wish; but it is now illegal to consume alcohol in the open, at or near a football stadium.

As a (relatively) liberal society, we have set out to regulate and control the production, sale and consumption of alcohol, rather than prohibit it altogether. The ordinary (adult) citizen is free to drink as much alcohol as he can buy, provided that he does not misbehave under its use, for example by being disorderly or violent, or by committing specified offences such as being drunk in charge of a firearm or driving under the influence of alcohol. What he does at home, at the Rugby Club, or even in the police canteen is pretty much his own affair. (Although the police officer is subject to the discipline code – which appears to have been suspended for Inspector Morse.)

If the drinker's actions primarily damage himself we tolerate them, although we may disapprove. If they damage or could damage others, we stop them – or try to do so. We believe that the citizen should be treated as a rational adult, and that the police are not entitled to assume that he has broken the law, even if the temptation is there. Thus, the police are not entitled to set up road-blocks near public houses at closing time, and stop and breathalyse any motorist leaving the pub, purely on the (statistically reasonable) assumption that they are likely to catch at least one or two motorists who are over the limit. The police should only stop and breathalyse anyone whom they have independent evidence to suspect of the offence in question. Whether or not it is a serious moral offence for a police officer to exceed his powers in this area, in the interests of preventing accidents on the roads, I leave it for the reader to judge. Have I phrased that problem in a leading manner? Very probably!

Other countries, with different traditions, take a different approach. In the Moslem world, alcohol is forbidden because the Prophet forbade it. In the stricter Moslem countries its use is forbidden for everyone, believers and infidels alike. The United States of America, abandoning liberal values for a quasi-religious puritanism, attempted for a lengthy period to prohibit alcohol, and the prohibition era became a byword for gangsterism and corruption.

No law can be effectively enforced if the majority breaks or ignores it, and the police will always find it easier to enforce law than morality – provided that the two can be separated.

Drugs

The whole issue of drugs is deeply confusing, and the approach which the police should take is not at all clear.

☐ Drugs, like alcohol, have been with us for a long time.
☐ Drugs, like alcohol, can be legally or illegally produced.
☐ Drugs, like alcohol, can have both proper and improper uses.

However, whereas the use of alcohol is tolerated within a highly controlled framework, the United Kingdom has reversed its traditional policy in regard to drugs, and attempted to prohibit their production, sale and use – even where the effect is likely to be deleterious only or at least primarily for the person who has chosen to buy and use them. In other words, we are attempting to control the self-regarding behaviour of the citizen in his own home.

An enduring problem

Has this policy been successful? In other words, are the forces of law and order, police and customs officers, winning the so-called war against drugs? Clearly not; and the size of the seizures quoted as an indication of police or customs success could equally prove that they are finding the same or even a smaller proportion of the assets of an increasing problem.

The police view

In practice, both law and police recognize that it is inappropriate to prosecute an individual for the use of small amounts of a so-called soft drug such as marijuana; and a distinction is made between 'users' and 'sellers' of drugs, the former being tolerated, to some extent, and the latter pursued. This may be out of respect for Mill's very simple principle, or simply because the problem would otherwise be too great to be addressed. Whatever the reason, the present situation causes the police immense problems. Drug abuse is a major activity, and a difficult area to police effectively. After all, drugs represent a very good return on investment to the enterprising criminal (who may begin, like Howard Marks and other student suppliers, by regarding himself not as a criminal at all, but as a benefactor who is selflessly helping his friends achieve a better life). Drugs are easily grown or made, harvested or packaged, distributed, smuggled across national frontiers if necessary, and sold. Formal advertising would be rather counter-productive, and there are little or no legitimate business costs. Demand, as the economists would put it, is inelastic: the more you consume, the more you want. Possibilities for corrupting law enforcement officials are enormous. Bribery may be seen either as simply a necessary business expense, to be set off against profits just as tax would be, if the drugs baron paid any; or as an excellent opportunity for the necessary art of money-laundering. (Howard Marks invested in a dress shop, here as elsewhere showing the somewhat eccentric approach to crime of the graduate.)

However, it is not the Howard Marks of this world who cause the police the most problems, but rather the petty criminals who rob, burgle, forge and steal in order to feed their habit. Judging by the views expressed in police magazines, it is likely that many police officers would vote neither for the status quo nor total freedom, but for something in between.

The public view

Many people who would otherwise be regarded as law-abiding, tax-paying, house-owning, respectable members of society will at least have sampled drugs such as marijuana or cocaine. These people will include magistrates, lawyers, teachers and priests. A large proportion of our young people – some surveys indicate a majority of people between the ages of 16 and 25 – will have taken some illegal substance, such as the drugs mentioned above, crack, speed or ecstasy. In due course, the number of people who will at least have sampled drugs out of curiosity must include a significant minority of police officers – if it does not do so already.

The effects of drug addiction are not entirely clear. Some see any form of drug habit as leading inexorably to a miserable and early death, the life of the addict, to misapply Hobbes, being nasty, poor, brutish, solitary and short. Others differ, and point to chronic constipation as the major consequence of heroin addiction.

The moral view

To allow the legal use of drugs under controlled conditions is not necessarily to say that you approve of drug-taking and wish to encourage it. Toleration does not mean approval; and it would be consistent both with Mill and our policy on alcohol, if we altered our policy on drugs.

Conclusions?

Although all this seems to point towards the need to change an unenforceable policy, there are other arguments. Because a law is difficult to enforce is not a sufficient reason for saying that its intention should be abandoned; and there is a wide variety of opinion within the police service, as in society as a whole, as to what would constitute a moral and sensible policy on drugs. As always, ethics and practice overlap. We cannot effectively prohibit what the majority do, or what requires a disproportionate effort to police. Consider, for example, the 70 mile an hour speed limit on motorways. What is clear is that we have attempted to deal with the problem of drugs by a general policy of prohibition, and that the policy has not worked. Is there an acceptable alternative?

ACTIVITY

If you were in a position to enact a new policy in regard to the issue of drugs in your police area, what would it be?

Please note that although we have set this question locally, you would in reality have to consider the national context in which your local initiative occurred. If drug-taking were legal in Hampshire and vigorously policed in Wiltshire, we should expect a large number of Wiltshire drug-users to cross the border. Please consider the policy you would wish to see in your area, without considering the national context.

Options

☐ To maintain the status quo.
☐ To maintain and reinforce the present policy, by:
  — investing a greater effort in investigating the illegal use of drugs and prosecuting the offenders, with the use of both trained people and technology;
  — increasing efforts to educate young people in the dangers of drug abuse, by means of school visits and other police programmes;
  — contributing to any other efforts made by both local government and community to create a society in which drug-taking becomes less popular.
☐ To modify the policy of prohibition towards one of control, so that the production, sale and use of drugs is regulated and controlled, as for alcohol. In addition, drug addiction would be decriminalized, to the effect that registered addicts would be able to obtain what they needed from their doctor, rather than by theft or other illegal means.
☐ To remove all restrictions of any kind, on the production, sale and use of any drug.

Commentary

We have already touched upon some of the major issues in regard to drugs in our general discussion of the topic. This activity was intended to help you form your own conclusions. If it did not do that, it will at least have helped you shape your thoughts as to what you still need to know, research or consider. Drugs have certainly not been under-researched, and there is an enormous amount of literature on drugs and drugs policies.

PROTEST

Mill referred to the tyranny of the majority as a possibility even under a democratic system of government. Under any representative system, there must be times when the decision that the government has made is not quite the one that we would have chosen. The question then becomes: are we bound by it? Some people feel that they have a right to disobey or reject the law, and their behaviour must create a particular problem for those who are charged with its enforcement. A liberal democracy, other things being equal, will tolerate a greater extent and degree of protest than an autocratic government; and will offer a greater flexibility to its law enforcement officials in how to deal with events such as protests, demonstrations, and acts of civil disobedience motivated by conscience. Before I come to discuss in detail the issue of ethically-motivated protest, I need to clear away some conceptual undergrowth.

Why do people disobey or reject the law?

A. Where the criminal motive is dominant

Criminals disobey the law because they stand to gain personally from law-breaking – although, logically, they would not wish everyone else to follow suit. A thief may be just as indignant as anyone else if what he has stolen is stolen from him. A criminal disobeys but does not reject the law.

B. Where a political agenda applies

i. Rebellion
People may disobey or reject the law because they do not accept the legitimacy of the state which created it. As the title of this section declares, this goes beyond protest to rebellion. An example of such a group is the Irish Republican Army, which refuses to recognize the existence and legitimacy of Northern Ireland. When a significant number of people rejects the law to the extent of taking part in an armed rebellion against its representatives and killing them at every opportunity, this places an intolerable strain upon the notion of policing by consent, and if the government is to retain or reimpose control it must police by authority and probably by armed force.

Clearly, we have gone beyond protest; and the interesting question becomes whether or not one can preserve a liberal democracy against illiberal attack, without suspending or sacrificing the features which make the liberal democracy desirable in the first place.

Although we touch upon the difficulties of policing Northern Ireland in this book, it is not my intention to address those problems in detail. That would require another book. Clearly, Northern Ireland is very different to the rest of the United Kingdom, historically, constitutionally and socially, and it has its own history and tradition of policing. Officers of the Royal Ulster Constabulary face the normal practical and ethical dilemmas that face all police officers, and some others as well; and I shall use the history of policing the province to illustrate some general policing dilemmas with a particular force and poignancy. What I shall not attempt to do is to suggest that armed rebellion should be combated as if it were simply criminal activity on a larger scale. The IRA is not helpfully classified as simply a group of criminals or (purposeless) terrorists. It is, as its title suggests, an army. Its membership includes criminals and psychopaths, and its tactics show a mastery of terrorism linked to propaganda. Its motive is political. Let us recognize the enemy for what it is, and not falsely classify it for the purposes of our own propaganda.

ii. Political action

People may break the law because they wish to change government policy, or indeed change the government. Arthur Scargill, the leader of the National Union of Mineworkers, led his men out on strike in 1983 not so much to improve miners' pay and conditions, as to change government policy on closing pits. The strike involved law-breaking.

C. Where conscience intervenes

The conscientious objector objects to a particular law or action on moral grounds.

A classic example is the refusal of a Quaker or other religious person to participate in war. His aim is not so much to change government policy, as to indicate his right not to be bound by it.

In a liberal democracy private citizens may claim the right, in Thoreau's famous phrase, to be civilly disobedient. If we do not like a law, we may say so. If we choose not to accept it, then we may carry out a personal act of disobedience – but we must also accept the consequences. In 1854, David Thoreau refused to pay his taxes because he did not approve of the United States declaring war on Mexico; and he was sent to jail as a result. (Bathetically, his taxes were paid by a relative and he was released from jail after one day.) His argument, which has had a considerable moral influence on protest, was that the citizen has a higher duty than simply to obey the law: and that is to his conscience.

The importance of motive

If a citizen refuses to accept or disobeys a particular law, then we need to know why he has chosen to dispute its authority. If it is for personal gain then his behaviour is not only illegal but unethical. A burglar cannot claim that he is acting for ethical reasons. If the act of defiance or disobedience cannot benefit its perpetrator in any material sense – if, indeed, his behaviour is likely to cause him distress, suffering or hardship – then we shall be more inclined to accept its ethical motivation.

We will also be keenly interested to note the type of disobedience which is being practised. Gandhi developed the notion of passive resistance, and took the high moral ground in his ultimately successful campaign to make the British leave India. Violent and destructive protest gives the police a much clearer role, in that they have a more obvious reason to enforce the law, and more broken laws to enforce.

Is civil disobedience acceptable?

The answer to that depends upon your interpretation of the social contract which theoretically underpins the relationship between citizen and state. In practice, it may depend more upon the quantity and intensity of dissent than the arguments upon which that dissent is based. The degree of sophistication of a state may be judged by how it deals with dissent. Any state can tolerate a manageable amount of disobedience. No state can tolerate a wholesale rejection of its authority.

The unique role of the police

Police officers, by virtue of their choice of occupation, have given away the right to be civilly disobedient. A police officer may not disobey, flout, or openly question the law, whatever his private moral convictions. He may exercise discretion as to whether or not he enforces a particular law on a particular occasion; but his decision should not be based upon his estimation of the worthiness of the law in question. Suppose a police officer does not arrest a man who is smoking marijuana in the street, or committing some other potentially arrestable offence. If his reasoning is that to make an arrest would be to provoke a riot, then his decision not to exercise his powers would appear the right one. If his reasoning is that the law in question is a bad law and should not be enforced, then he is at fault, in that he is betraying the trust placed in him as an officer of the law.

Police officers fulfil a vital role in our constitution, in that it is their presence and actions which allow ordinary citizens to demonstrate their convictions. The good police officer knows how to police a protest or demonstration in such a way as to ensure that the demonstrators feel that they have had the opportunity to make their voices heard, that the minimum disruption is caused to normal business, and that at the end of the day everyone goes home peacefully. Unfortunately, peaceful demonstration may turn to violence or rioting, irrespective of police tactics; and in those circumstances it is clearly the duty of the police to fulfil their primary responsibility of restoring that public order without which normal life cannot function.

ACTIVITY

You are a police officer working in a coastal area of England from which live calves are exported to the continent to be slaughtered and sold as veal. A large number of local citizens believe this to be a cruel and unnecessary trade, and have set out to demonstrate their beliefs by protesting what is going on. Ideally, they would like to stop the exports dead. As a secondary objective, they are determined to publicize their views as strongly as they can and to win public support and eventually parliamentary action to their side.

As a police officer, you must enforce the law. There is no law against exporting calves, and the actions of the exporters are therefore purely legal. The actions of the other side are not. The favourite tactic of the protesters is to attempt to block the road leading to the docks from which the calves are exported. Blocking the Queen's Highway is an offence, and although as a police officer you have a variety of tactics at your disposal – you may cajole, persuade, and reason with the protesters as long as these tactics appear to have some likelihood of success – ultimately you must ensure that traffic may use the highway. That means that if necessary you must use force to clear it, even if it is blocked by non-violent and highly principled demonstrators, who are acting for a cause which appears to have public sympathy.

The dilemma is simply this. Do you, as a police service, allow your members to express their moral views, publicly and in uniform, about what is going on? Or do you tell them that their moral views are not a matter for public debate, and that they should keep silent?

What is your view on the correct force policy?

Commentary

Like all good dilemmas, this one has no model answer. In favour of open debate, you could argue that if we believe in policing by consent, then we want a thoughtful and well-informed police service, and not a set of robots in uniform. Reflective police officers will be capable of expressing their views in such a way as to add to the moral debate without unduly influencing it. Moreover, they will benefit from the relief of being able to say what they think, in a restrained and appropriate manner.

In favour of a silent force, it could be said that for the police to express their views officially, as it were, will give those views undue weight. Moreover, it creates a precedent. If the police express their views in one corner of the moral arena, why not elsewhere? That brings the police firmly on to the political pitch as players, and may take away something from the notion of their impartiality.

The traditional answer to this dilemma is that the police should not officially express a political view; and it is interesting to note that during the veal export demonstrations of 1995 and 1996, the Essex police held to the traditional vow of silence, whereas the Chief Constable of Sussex expressed his personal abhorrence at the veal trade, while reaffirming his duty to preserve the rule of law. Is there a right answer? Not necessarily. Ethics is about making defendable choices, and both positions were defensible.

9
THE RELIGIOUS DIMENSION

WHAT IS RELIGION?

The Polish philosopher Leszek Kolakowski (1981) defines religion as
'The socially established worship of the eternal reality.'
  Commonly, religions involve:

- [ ] A belief in a God or Gods.
- [ ] A doctrine or dogma.
- [ ] A priesthood.
- [ ] An act of collective worship.
- [ ] A moral code which includes prohibitions.

Not all of what would commonly be accepted as religions match the
whole of this list. For example, Buddhism has no God, but would
appear a religion by other criteria. Islam does not advocate a separate
priesthood, as in Anglicanism and other faiths. Hindus have many
Gods, and Hinduism has been called more a way of life than a religion.
Some religions are more relaxed about their prohibitions than others;
but all would appear to prohibit something.

The essence of religion

We have been offering a sociological definition of religion – a
recognition of its constituent elements, but not its essence. It is as if
we were to describe a clock by enumerating its working parts, but to
forget to point out its fundamental purpose: to tell the time. The
essence of a religion is to take part in an act of collective worship with

fellow believers. Religion is about faith, fellowship and forgiving. It is not simply a moral code.

Belief and behaviour

It is possible to be a moral atheist, or an immoral Christian, Buddhist, or any other religious adherent. The acceptance of a religious faith is neither necessary nor sufficient to be a good person. An atheist or agnostic may claim a moral basis for his behaviour, which has nothing to do with religion. Humanists, in fact, make precisely that claim. However, it would be unhistorical to argue that ethics and religion are unrelated. Most ethical codes originated in religious teachings.

'Man is a mixture of generous and selfish impulses.'

Jean Jacques Rousseau

The motives for our behaviour are complicated, and cannot be reduced to simple statements of abstract rationality or religious faith. Why do we attempt to do what is good? For a mixture of reasons, as Rousseau suggested – and none knew better than he. It would be as foolish to assume that an ethical but unreligious person acts in a good way because he is convinced by the logic of humanism, as to assume that a religious person acts ethically directly and only for the reason that it is the path to Heaven.

Need morality be prohibitive?

How attractive it would be if there were no clash between pleasure and morality, and what we wanted to do was also what we should! All too often, to do what is right conflicts with how we would behave naturally. Some writers would have us believe that morality is a western rather than universal concept; the product of a particular stage in the evolution of a particular society, to be associated with other depressing concepts like Puritanism and the Protestant Work Ethic. In her influential work *Coming of Age in Samoa* (1971) Margaret Mead presents an idyllic picture of life on an island in the South Seas, in which beautiful and largely unclothed adolescents grow up in a society which has very few restrictions, and in which sexual experimentation is encouraged. But Margaret Mead does not give us the full picture, and what she does say may not have been accurate. Anthropologists can be

misled by the societies they study, particularly if they are disposed to
look for a certain state of affairs in the first place; and later observers
discovered that Margaret Mead was wrong about Samoa. There were
sexual taboos in place which she missed or ignored, and the other
prohibitions upon the free behaviour of Samoans were as restricting as
the inhibitions in place in any other society.

Margaret Mead was not the first exponent of the myth of the noble
savage. Diderot and Rousseau had been there before her. It is a
recurring human theme to believe that somewhere there is a better
(happier; more harmonious; less frictional) society than our own, and to
see that society as free from our prohibitions and inhibitions. But even
the supposedly freest of societies has restrictions (read any account of
life in a Utopian commune) and where laws do not exist, they are
replaced by group pressures or the personality of the leader. An
anarchist community might lack uniformed police officers, but would
certainly be subject to Mill's 'moral coercion of public opinion'. We are
entitled to conclude, not that the concept of a prohibitive morality is
universal, but that we have yet to discover a culture without one.

SHOULD THE LAW PROTECT RELIGION?

Salman Rushdie, blasphemy and the police

English law defines blasphemy as speaking against the Christian
religion, and does not protect others. This anomaly has caused a strong
debate, well argued in Commission for Racial Equality (1990a).

What are we to do about peoples' religious sensitivities?

Options would appear to be as follows:

☐ To maintain the status quo and the privileged position of
Christianity.
☐ To expand the definition of the offence of blasphemy so that it
might be applied to other religions. This is the view taken by the
Church of England, and defended by Lord Justice Scarman in a
House of Lords verdict in 1977, as follows:

> In an increasingly plural society such as that of modern Britain it is
> necessary not only to respect the differing religious beliefs, feelings
> and practices of all but also to protect them from scurrility,
> vilification, ridicule and contempt.

☐ To prosecute for another offence, rather than blasphemy. Professor Simon Lee compares blasphemy and incitement to religious hatred, and argues that the latter offence offers the possibility of assuaging religious sensitivities.

☐ To abolish the offence of blasphemy altogether, with no substitute encouraged. Let free speech prevail!

None of these options appears wholly satisfactory, and none of them would solve the problem of Salman Rushdie and his *fatwa*. Suppose it were an offence to blaspheme against any established religion, in Great Britain. The fact that an offence exists does not mean that a prosecution would necessarily be mounted; nor that it would necessarily be successful; nor that those who had been outraged by the blasphemy would accept the suitability of charge, conviction and sentence, and refrain from any reprisal of their own.

Thoughts

I would suggest that in a liberal democracy:

1. We would be unlikely to extend the range of the law in regard to what some, perhaps the majority, would see an unnecessary restriction of free speech.
2. If we did extend the range of the law, we should probably attach a light penalty to such an offence.
3. Such a penalty would not be considered adequate by those offended in the first place.

In another publication, the Commission for Racial Equality (1990b) accepts that the law must apply to all, and points to the important role of the courts. I quote:

> The courts are located at the point of intersection between the state and society as well as between the law and the individual.... The courts ... tease out the limits of diversity and tolerance.
>
> Britain cannot allow separate legal systems for different communities without violating the fundamental principles of common citizenship and equality before the law. However, it can and should accommodate acceptable cultural differences without violating these principles.
>
> Parliament and the courts have also indicated several broad principles for deciding which ethnic practices are unacceptable. The Female Circumcision Act 1985 bans all forms of female circumcision.

Polygamy constitutes the crime of bigamy under the Offences Against the Person Act 1961.... In a number of cases in which the question of respect for minority cultural practices has been specifically raised, English judges have appealed to notions of reasonableness, public policy, principles of humanity, Britain's commitment to international conventions on human rights, and repugnance to the conscience of the court (p. 72).

Comment

What the Commission for Racial Equality understands by pluralism has much in common with what Mill understood by liberal democracy. A state which recognizes the virtues of freedom and tolerance, and which does not exert a tyrannical power over any of its citizens, is a state whose citizenship will be highly prized.

ABSOLUTISM AND PLURALISM

'I believe in all religions': Senior Indian Police Officer (Brahmin).

Can a society exist with more than one major religion? In other words, is a multi-faith society possible? According to Canon Keith Walker of the Winchester diocese, Christians have three options:

1. **Exclusivism**. Christ is the way, the truth and the life. There is no other possible way to God. Therefore, by implication, Christians have a duty to evangelize, and there must be a limit to the tolerance they extend to other faiths.
2. **Pluralism**. All religions are of equal value. (Whether or not the definition of religion would include what are normally referred to as cults, is a point to be debated. As it stands, if we refer to all religions without further clarification, we would appear to be including cults.)
3. **Inclusivism**. For a Christian, the way to God is through Christ. Love is the key. Inclusivism accepts that there may be other ways to God for people who are not Christians. By implication, evangelism is not a good thing, except with people who have no faith.

. . . .

Discussion

Exclusivism is a harsh doctrine. What of the people who could never have heard Jesus' message? Are they condemned to Hell or, if we are feeling slightly more generous, Limbo? And if Christians do set out to convert others, what if they do not want to be converted?

Pluralism is a wishy-washy doctrine which sounds dangerously close to moral relativism. What does it really mean? That there is no difference between religions? That they all have certain features in common? Or that, on the whole, it is a good thing if people line themselves up with some sort of recognizable code, as long as it does not contradict other peoples' fundamental values too seriously?

In a society which places a high value on tolerance, it is tempting not to probe too far the comforting but unproven assumption that the world's major faiths have much in common. That might sound plausible: but as soon as we begin to look at any religion in depth, we shall discover that it has significant differences to other creeds. The philosopher Arthur C Danto (1987) makes a thoughtful comparison between Christianity, Hinduism and Buddhism, and claims that the ethics upon which they are based cannot necessarily be reconciled. He argues against the possibility of a universal ethic, quoting Max Weber in his book *The Religion of India* (1992) that the caste system does not allow for one set of ethics even among Hindus:

> There is no universally valid ethic, but only a strict status compartmentalisation of private and social ethic, disregarding the few general and ritualistic prohibitions (particularly the killing of cows). This was of great moment. The doctrine of *karma* deduced from the principle of compensation for previous deeds in the world, not only explained the caste organization but the rank order of divine, human and animal beings of all degree. Hence it provided for the coexistence of different ethical codes for different status groups which not only differed widely but were often in sharp conflict.... [Men] were as unlike as man and animal.

Danto goes on:

> To be sure, the failure to establish a system of ethics that is held to be universally valid has its compensations. It leads to a measure of toleration.

Inclusivism sounds interesting, but does it make sense? Jesus did not qualify His message, but addressed mankind in general. Is inclusivism

THE RELIGIOUS DIMENSION 207

logically defensible, or simply a useful position for someone who lives and works in a multi-faith society and does not wish to stir up a hornets' nest? Since that is the position of the police officer, I see no reason to dispute its usefulness – provided that we do not equate it with moral relativism.

India, which as we all know is a religiously divided society in which inter-community strife can be highly destructive, has a secular constitution, and its police force embodies and upholds the secular virtues of impartiality. Sikh police officers do not necessarily police Sikh citizens, nor Hindus the Hindu. The police need not be irreligious, but they must be neutral.

The answer to my question is yes. A multi-faith society is possible: but no one, to quote Terry Waite, said that it would be easy. And that is the end of my comments on religion.

10
PUTTING IT TOGETHER

Man is born free, but everywhere he is in chains.

J J Rousseau

Philosophers have sought to understand the world. The point is to change it.

Karl Marx

Perhaps this book will be understood only by someone who has himself already had the thoughts that are expressed within it – or at least similar thoughts. So it is not a textbook. Its purpose would be achieved if it gave pleasure to one person who read and understood it....

I do not wish to judge how far my efforts coincide with those of other philosophers. Indeed, what I have written here makes no claim to novelty in detail, and the reason why I give no sources is that it is a matter of indifference to me whether the thoughts that I have had been anticipated by someone else.

Ludwig Wittgenstein, Preface to *Tractatus Logico-Philosophicus*

Real police dilemmas, like the dilemmas faced in other occupations, are not as tidy as in some of our examples.

Real dilemmas are often protracted, complex and incomplete. They may well be bound up with court cases. If they are, there is almost always a lengthy delay between the event which forms the basis for the dilemma, and its legal resolution.

Real dilemmas occur in an historical and political context. Thus, if a police constable is accused of neglect of duty, some of those who support him will not do so because they believe that what he did was right. They may take good care not to ask themselves whether or not what he did was right, lest a negative judgement cloud their actions. They will support him because it is their duty, as colleagues or official representatives, to do so.

Real dilemmas may be clouded by financial considerations that are seen as outweighing 'moral' issues: although in reality how much you spend upon solving a problem is as much a moral decision as anything else.

Bearing these factors in mind, let us look at a police dilemma as it develops over time, and consider both its tactical and strategic implications. This dilemma is essentially a challenge to police leadership. If this book has had an effect, it will be in that the full challenge is recognized.

IT WAS AN ACCIDENT

1. A young police officer is driving a police car back to the station having issued a summons. He is instructed by radio from the duty controller, Elaine Noar-Hill, to respond to a 999 call in another part of town, where there is reported to be a domestic emergency. He puts on the siren and drives there as fast as possible, exceeding the speed limit where he believes it to be safe to do so under the circumstances. Siren blaring, he crosses the traffic lights in the centre of town just as they have changed from amber to red, and hits another car making a legitimate manoeuvre. The driver of the other car, a district nurse on duty named Janet Selbourne, is killed. Constable James Hawkley stops to deal with the road traffic accident which he has caused, and never responds to the original emergency call.

2. Subsequent investigation shows that the 999 call was made by a distraught housewife, Mrs Vera Steep. Mrs Steep feared that her husband Johannes, who was about to enter the house and was clearly very much the worse for drink, was about to attack her, as he had done many times before. As it happened, Mr Steep did not do so. He walked up his drive shouting threats against his wife, but after he had opened the door collapsed in an alcoholic stupor on the floor of their small hallway, where he slept for several hours. During that period Mrs Steep moved out to a battered women's refuge, as she had long considered doing. She is now living with another man, with whom she had been having an affair since soon after marrying Johannes Steep.

3. Constable Hawkley is suspended from duty pending an official investigation. During his suspension, Constable Hawkley asks for stress counselling. It is offered and accepted. Although the counsellor, Amanda Alton, is employed by the police service, she refuses to discuss what Constable Hawkley told her about the road traffic accident with the police officer who is responsible for investigating it. She claims that a counsellor is entitled to offer confidentiality and that this was the basis for her conversation with Constable Hawkley.

. . . .

4. Constable Hawkley is charged with causing death by dangerous driving, and remains on suspension until his case is heard. During this period his mental health deteriorates, and he is treated for depression by his GP. Many months later, Constable Hawkley is convicted of causing death by dangerous driving, despite his defence that he is exempt from the need to obey a red light since he is responding to an emergency, as cited under Section 87 of the Road Traffic Regulation Act.

5. The judge imposes a suspended sentence, saying that Hawkley has already suffered enough. There is outrage in the tabloid press over the sentence, which is considered much too lenient and as showing that there is one rule for the ordinary citizen and another for the police. The brother of the dead nurse makes a statement from prison that no punishment is too much for the police constable who caused his sister's death. The nurse's fiance, on the other hand, is quoted as saying that in his opinion it was a tragic accident, for which the constable should not torture himself. The chief constable exercises his discretion and does not dismiss Constable Hawkley from the force, but offers him continuing employment.

6. Constable Hawkley officially returns to duty, but never actually goes out on patrol from the station as a working police officer. He seeks early retirement from the force on medical grounds, claiming that the accident has caused him irreversible depression and that he is suffering from post-traumatic stress disorder. He can no longer contemplate driving a police car, nor responding to any emergency. The Police Federation takes up his case, and points out that he had received no special training as a police driver before the fatal accident occurred. The police force had a duty of care towards this officer and failed to guard his interests. In due course, and by administrative decision, Constable Hawkley retires early on grounds of ill-health, on almost a full pension.

Reflection

- ☐ Who was to blame for the accident? (Please distinguish between legal and moral responsibility.)
- ☐ What are the general ethical issues that arise in this study, and how would you resolve them?
- ☐ How could you make sure that these circumstances were never repeated?

Analysis

Rather than subject this saga to the usual dispassionate and objective scrutiny, let us make it the basis for a dialogue.

Q. 'Who was to blame for the road traffic accident?'
A. 'Clearly we must first cite Constable Hawkley, since he ignored a red light.'
Q. 'Was there any contributory negligence by another driver?'
A. 'Possibly. However, since Nurse Selbourne is dead and there were no witnesses, we shall never know whether or not she contributed to the accident by her driving. To give credit to Constable Hawkley, he accepted total responsibility for what occurred and did not seek to blame anyone else.'
Q. 'Were there any mitigating circumstances?'
A. 'Plenty. First, Constable Hawkley was responding to an emergency ...'
Q. 'Hold on. We now know that there was no emergency.'
A. 'Yes, there was. Mrs Steep dialled 999 and reported that she was about to be attacked. What do you call that, if not an emergency?'
Q. 'Yes – but she wasn't attacked, was she?'
A. 'No. But it was reasonable at the time, both for her to call the police, and for the police to treat it as an emergency.'
Q. 'Couldn't the police operator on duty have talked to Mrs Steep, and found out a bit more before he despatched the patrol car?'
A. 'Have you ever worked in a police control room? Obviously not. That isn't how it works. The controller's job is to check basic details and decide upon the immediate response. In this case, once Mrs Noar-Hill knew that Mrs Steep was in danger, she had to send help. Once the police officer arrived, he could assess the situation. There was nothing more the controller could do. Are you suggesting that Mrs Noar-Hill should have kept Mrs Steep talking until she had proof that her husband had attacked her?'
Q. 'No.'
A. 'Good. Besides, the controller didn't know that Constable Hawkley would hit Janet Selbourne's car. Elaine did nothing wrong. May I go back to where we were?'
Q. 'Yes'.
A. 'Thank you. First, Constable Hawkley was responding to an emergency. Secondly, he had to get to the incident as fast as possible.'
Q. 'As fast as safely possible, surely. What's the point of adding to your problems? Isn't one emergency enough, at a time?'
A. 'There's no need to be flippant. The officer had to get to the incident quickly. For all he knew, life was in danger and seconds were vital.'

Q. 'But he caused a death by driving recklessly.'
A. 'The fact is that he was under pressure to carry out his duty quickly. That is a mitigating circumstance. It doesn't exonerate what he did. In any case, it wasn't reckless driving, but a few seconds' misjudgement. That isn't the same thing.'
Q. 'Oh?'
A. 'Finally, Constable Hawkley didn't actually break the law.'
Q. 'What do you mean? He disobeyed the lights! What's that, if it isn't breaking the law? You're not going to tell me that police drivers are above the law, are you?'
A. 'No.'
Q. 'I'm glad not to hear it.'
A. 'The Road Traffic Regulations Act allows certain legal exemptions to police drivers ...'
Q. 'Yes? You were going to add something?'
A. 'Provided that they drive with due care.'
Q. 'So you are above the law.'
A. 'No. The law recognizes competing priorities, that's all. A certain level of risk may be justified. But it has to be justified in court, if necessary.'
Q. 'And what precautions do you take to minimise the adverse effects of your behaviour?'
A. 'I'm sorry? You're being rather abstract. What do you mean?'
Q. 'What I mean is this. You allow police drivers to speed, or take other risks on occasion.'
A. 'For good reason, yes.'
Q. 'For good reason. And you obviously make sure that their cars are well serviced and maintained, so that you have made every reasonable effort to prevent an accident. For example, the brakes are in first-class order.'
A. 'Yes. They should be.'
Q. 'They should be. And the drivers are specially trained.'
A. 'Some of them, yes.'
Q. 'Some of them. Was Constable Hawkley specially trained in high-risk driving?'
A. 'We were satisfied that he was a competent driver.'
Q. 'That's not what I asked. Was Constable Hawkley – '
A. 'No.'
Q. 'I see.'
A. 'We had to respond to an emergency. He was the only police officer available who was near and had transport.'
Q. 'Couldn't you have told him not to take any risks?'
A. 'Now we're back to where we started. This was a 999 call. An emergency. Constable Hawkley chose how to respond. No controller

could tell him how to drive. Police officers are trained to use their discretion.'

Q. 'Even if it risks life?'

A. 'It depends on the risk.'

Q. 'All right, let's talk about risk. You had cause to believe that Mrs Steep was in danger.'

A. 'Because of the telephone call.'

Q. 'So you sent an emergency response. Tell me, what was Constable Hawkley supposed to do when he arrived at the scene?'

A. 'To use his initiative, assess the situation, and decide what to do.'

Q. 'Could he expect a particular pattern of events?'

A. 'He couldn't expect anything, if you want a precise prediction of what was likely to happen. Every situation that a police officer faces is different.'

Q. 'But there are patterns to events, if you sit back and look at them. For example, how often is an emergency response really necessary?'

A. 'What do you mean?'

Q. 'I mean, how often is a supposed emergency a real one? How often does the police officer arrive just in time to stop someone from taking the breadknife to his wife, or jumping out of the window, or drinking the paraffin? How much do seconds really count?'

A. 'It's impossible to tell. But I know this much. When you call for a police officer, you want one. As soon as they can get there.'

Q. 'Isn't it true that in many cases the police don't do very much – especially in domestic disputes? When they arrive, people simply pack it in?'

A. 'Sometimes. When they arrive. What are you trying to say? That because the drama fizzles out – sometimes – when the police appear, a fast response wasn't necessary? Or that we should somehow be able to know what sort of risk we can take in driving to an incident, before we have any confirmed knowledge about what is really going on? It isn't like that!'

According to the Road Traffic Regulation Act Section 87:

No statutory provision imposing a speed limit on vehicles shall apply to any vehicle on an occasion when it is being used for fire brigade, ambulance, or police purposes, if the observance of that provision would be likely to hinder the use of the vehicle for the purpose for which it is being used on that occasion.

Comment

As you can see, this dialogue could go on almost indefinitely. Q wants to find out the truth, whereas A wishes to put the case for the police – or at least to limit the damage caused to the police's reputation in this scenario.

We are right to be concerned about the whys and wherefores of police speeding, since a death has occurred as a result of it – with the irony that the driver's intention was to protect life. However, the case does not end there. It may be tempting to confine our scrutiny to what is immediately to hand, but there are other issues, as Q was attempting to uncover.

In both the Hillsborough and Dunblane tragedies, senior police officers were subsequently officially criticized for taking too narrow an interpretation of their duties. Good leadership requires that the senior officer accepts his full responsibilities. In this case, there are issues about how the police are organized, equipped and trained to do their work. There is also an extremely knotty problem about stress, early retirement and pensions, which raises profound issues about what is right or wrong. These problems require both tactical and strategic solutions.

POLICE ETHICS AND THE FUTURE

Much of the emphasis of this book has been upon the individual police officer, the problems he faces, and how he may better resolve them. Qualities of conscience and character have been put first. I shall conclude by suggesting some organizational reforms which I believe would assist the individual police officer in his efforts to be and do better. There seems little point in writing something so bland that it will offend no one. Nor can I prove in advance that the reforms I suggest would achieve the advantages I predict for them. The alternative is to say nothing, to which I am disinclined.

Police doctrine

The bedrock of British policing is that we police by consent. This doctrine is nowhere authoritatively defined. It needs to be, since it is an ethic which must affect all police decision making. Here as elsewhere, the police need to be able to articulate and apply doctrine.

A national police service

The creation of a national police service would allow a higher standard of professionalism to be achieved, provided it were linked to other reforms. The present arrangement, whereby chief officers exercise an almost feudal power, encouraging or hindering moves towards organizational reform as the mood takes them, needs to be changed. Its supposed advantages are often in reality disadvantageous. For example, using the convention that chief constables have autonomy, some make great changes to how things are done in their area. Conversely, others do not. Both cannot be right.

National standards

The police service needs to set national standards for the behaviour it expects, linked to both ethical and disciplinary codes: the former aspirational and the latter punitive. The 1992 police ethical code is a good place to start. It should be correlated to the United Nations and European police codes, and its purpose declared.

Debating ethics

The gentlemanly model for a profession is out of date, but some of its features could be adapted to police needs. There is a need for a small, dynamic and effective police institute to discuss and review ethical dilemmas for the benefit of working police officers. The less bureaucratic this becomes, the better. It should not be funded by public money, and might even be sponsored. The police are an honourable body of men and women who contribute to the quality of life in the United Kingdom.

The impetus to raise standards from within must be encouraged.

RECOMMENDED READING

(Some of these sources are referred to in the text, by author and date of publication.)

Barry, Brian (1965) *Political Argument*, Routledge, London.
A good exposition of the differences between want-regarding and ideal-regarding principles, and their implications for the state.

Bergson, Henri, (1967) *Time and Free Will*, Unwin, London.
Are we responsible for our actions? Bergson (who wrote this book when he was 26, and never bettered it) distinguishes between the duration and intensity of our emotions, and points to the significance of this in analysing when, how, and why we make decisions, and our degree of responsibility for them. For those who enjoy classifying people, he is an intuitionist.

Bok, Sissela (1978) *Lying: Moral Choice in Public and Private Life*, Harvester Press, Brighton.
An excellent read.

Bok, Sissela (1986) *Secrets: On the Ethics of Concealment and Revelation*, Oxford University Press, Oxford.
This covers much of the same ground as the same author's *Lying* (*op. cit.*).

Bonifacio, Philip (1991) *The Psychological Effects of Police Work: A Psychodynamic Approach*, Plenum Press, New York.

Camus, Albert (1965) *The Outsider*, Penguin, Harmondsworth.
The outsider recognizes that others will not understand his morality, but still wants to be understood. Unlike Socrates, he is not prepared to accept the logic of the state in its punishment of his actions. How do we police the outsider? How do we police the outsider in ourselves?

Camus, Albert (1962) *The Rebel*, Penguin, Harmondsworth.
Camus analyses the justification for rebellion and rebellious violence. The actions of the tyrannicides who assassinated leading representatives of the Russian autocracy in the nineteenth century were, as they concluded themselves, both necessary and inexcusable. It was right that they did what they did; and it was right that they paid for their acts with their lives.

Commission for Racial Equality (1990a) *Law, Blasphemy and the Multi-Faith Society*, CRE, London.

Commission for Racial Equality (1990b) *Britain: A Plural Society*, CRE, London.

Crawshaw, Ralph, (1994) *Human Rights and the Theory and Practice of Policing*, The Human Rights Centre, University of Essex, Colchester. This is a short and profound paper in a series on human rights, in which the author drafts a general theory of policing.

Danto, Arthur C (1987) *Mysticism and Morality: Oriental Thought and Moral Philosophy*, Columbia University Press, New York.

Delattre, Edwin (1989) *Character and Cops: Ethics in Policing*, American Enterprise Institute for Public Policy Research, Washington DC.
An influential view on police ethics from an American practitioner.

Devlin, Patrick (1963) *The Enforcement of Morals*, Oxford University Press, Oxford.
The Hart-Devlin debate on morals and the role of the state in enforcing them is seminal to our understanding in this area. It is well summarized by Lee (qv). To some extent it repeats the nineteenth century debate between the liberal John Stuart Mill (Hart) and the conservative James Fitzjames Stephen (Devlin). Since it is 35 years since Devlin and Hart engaged each other, it may be time for others to enter the ring and fight round three.

Eysenck, H J, (1986) *The Decline and Fall of the Freudian Empire*, Penguin, London.

Goffman, Irving (1970) *Strategic Interaction*, Basil Blackwell, Oxford.

Greenhill, Norman, (1985) in Thackrah, N (ed.) *Contemporary Policing*, Sphere, London.

Gudjonsson, Gisli, (1992) *The Psychology of Interrogations, Confessions, and Testimony*, Wiley, Chichester.

Hart, H L A, (1963) *Law, Liberty and Morality*, Oxford University Press, Oxford.
See Devlin.

Hart, H L A, (1968) *Punishment and Responsibility: Essays in the Philosophy of Law*, Clarendon Press, Oxford.

Herrigel, Eugen (1990) *Zen in the Art of Archery*, Penguin, Harmondsworth.
Herrigel apprenticed himself to a Japanese master bowman, and was surprised by his teaching methods. The message of Zen is that if you do not know what to do, you cannot learn it; but that you must still work at what you cannot understand. Can we apply this to ethics?

Howard, Michael (1990) *British Intelligence in the Second World War Volume 5: Strategic Deception*, HMSO, London.
The end can justify the means.

Keegan, John (1976) *The Face of Battle*, Penguin Books, Harmondsworth.

Kelly, George A, (1963) *Theory of Personality: The Psychology of Personal Constructs*, W W Norton, New York.
George Kelly's model of man as a scientist who seeks to find out more and more about the world by a philosophy of constructive alternativism sounds jargon-laden and unuseful. In fact, his construction is clear, elegant and comprehensive, and gives us back the responsibility for our actions which Freud attempted to remove.

Kierkegaard, Soren (1971) *Either/Or*, (two volumes), Princeton University Press, New Jersey.
No one could say that the great Dane is an easy read. Why write a sentence when you can write a book – or, better still, fill a shelf with them? This extraordinary work contrasts the aesthetic, ethical and religious perspectives on life through the multiple personality of the author, writing under various pseudonyms. Kierkegaard believed that we reach an ethical stage in life, but cannot stay there. The last stage must be religious.

Kleinig, John (1996) *The Ethics of Policing*, Cambridge University Press, Cambridge.

A comprehensive and very detailed analysis of police ethics by an Australian scholar at the John Jay College of Criminal Justice, New York, to which this book is intended as complementary.

Lee, Simon (1986) *Law and Morals: Warnock, Gillick and Beyond*, Oxford University Press, Oxford.
Simon Lee is professor of jurisprudence at the University of Belfast, and an English Roman Catholic. The *Church Times* stated that this book 'is a model of economic yet lucid prose and well-disciplined argument.'

Kolakowski, Leszek (1981) *Religion*, Fontana Modern Masters, London.

Levi, Michael (1995) 'Covert policing and the investigation of "organised fraud": the English experience in international context', in Jinhaut, C and Marx G T (eds.) *Undercover Police Surveillance in Comparative Perspective*, Kluwer, London.

Magee, Bryan (1968) *Popper*, Fontana Modern Masters, London.
A very readable account of an immensely influential philosopher.

Mead, Margaret (1971) *Coming of Age in Samoa*, William Morrow, USA.

Mitchell, Basil (1967) *Law, Morality and Religion in a Secular Society*, Oxford University Press, Oxford.
A good addition to the Hart-Devlin debate.

Parkinson, C. Northcote, (1958) *Parkinson's Law: or The Pursuit of Progress*, John Murray, London.
Why read any other book on management? Work *does* expand to fill the time available for its completion, and there is a danger that excessive time devoted to studying ethics will simply illustrate the continuing validity of the law of diminishing returns. My law on communications would be this: written communication expands in inverse proportion to its value.

Pollock, Joycelyn M (1994) *Ethics in Crime and Justice: Dilemmas and Decisions*, Wadsworth, California.
The writer has a clear mind, and is particularly good on analysing practical problems from a variety of ethical perspectives. Her framework includes Ethical formalism (Kant); The Ethics of Virtue; Religious ethics; Utilitarianism; and Egoism. See, for example, her

220 BETTER POLICE ETHICS

analysis of the morality of drug abuse (p. 82). One reason I have not adopted her method in this book is my desire not to overegg the pudding.

Duc de la Rochefoucauld (1959) *Maxims*, Penguin, Harmondsworth.

Rowse, A L (1964) *Christopher Marlowe: a Biography*, Macmillan, London.
Dr Faustus' pact with the devil Mephistopheles, whereby Faustus will sell his soul provided that Mephistopheles will provide him with the opportunity to find out everything he wants to know, makes Faustus the informant to Mephistopheles as handler. Or is it the other way around? Marlowe, the scholar, poet, playwright, homosexual, atheist, secret agent and victim, is uniquely placed to understand and portray the morality of bargaining and deception.

Ryan, Alan (1970) *The Philosophy of the Social Sciences*, Macmillan, London.
Alan Ryan has also written on John Stuart Mill and the English liberal tradition. His work is always short, elegant and profound.

Schopenhauer, Arthur (1970) *Essays and Aphorisms*, Penguin, Harmondsworth.
'If the immediate and direct purpose of our life is not suffering then our existence is the most ill-adapted to its purpose in the world: for it is absurd to suppose that the endless affliction of which the world is everywhere full, and which arises out of the need and distress pertaining essentially to life, should be purposeless and purely accidental. Each individual misfortune, to be sure, seems an exceptional occurrence; but misfortune in general is the rule.'
To read Schopenhauer is to live Dostoyevsky's maxim: 'The thought of suicide has helped me through many a long night.'

Scruton, Roger (1996) *Animal Rights and Wrongs*, Demos, London.
Roger Scruton is the former professor of aesthetics at Birkbeck College, London, and a philosopher and controversialist. This book is a sustained and consistently argued polemic against what he sees as the philosophical inconsistencies and inadequacies of the Animal Rights enthusiasts and their intellectual leader, Peter Singer, the Professor of Ethics at Melbourne University. In laying out his own stall, Scruton gives his overall ethical position. His chapter on the rational basis of moral judgement reviews the moral law and advocates virtue, sympathy

and piety as moral criteria. An academic dog-fight (if you will forgive the expression) is always good fun, and this is a good read.

Stephen, James Fitzjames (1967) *Liberty Equality Fraternity*, Cambridge University Press, Cambridge.
A Victorian judge, historian of the criminal law and Indian law reformer, Stephen was the earliest and the most vigorous critic of John Stuart Mill's 'very simple principle' that we can easily and practicably distinguish between acts which harm ourselves, and acts which harm others, and that the state should confine its intentions to preventing the latter.

Townshend, Charles (1986) *Britain's Civil Wars: Counterinsurgency in the Twentieth Century*, Faber and Faber, London.
This and Professor Townshend's other works explore police and army officers' decisions in time of armed insurrection.

Villers, Leon (1918) *The War on Workers*, The Workers' Press, Melbourne.

Villiers, Peter (1993) *Structured Workshops for Developing Leadership*, Gower, Aldershot.

Villiers, Peter (1995) *Without Fear or Favour: Policing a Changing Democracy*, UNISON Education, London.

Weber, Max (1992) *The Religion of India*, Bowker, USA.

Winch, Peter (1990) *The Idea of a Social Science and its Relation to Philosophy*, Routledge, London.
Short, clear and profound, this book is a little nugget. Winch distinguishes between laws and rules, and suggests that social behaviour is governed by the latter more than the former. Our physical actions are governed by the laws of science, of which we may have no understanding, or even be aware. Our behaviour only makes sense within the context of rules, which require understanding and application. Thus, to play soccer we must know the rules, or have someone interpret and apply them for us. Police officers are supposed to apply the law. In fact, they apply the rules.

INDEX